I0878539

More Than This

More Than This

poems

DAVID KIRBY

Louisiana State University Press Baton Rouge

Published by Louisiana State University Press
Copyright © 2019 by David Kirby
All rights reserved
Manufactured in the United States of America
First printing

Designer: Barbara Neely Bourgoyne
Typeface: Fournier MT Pro
Printer and binder: Sheridan Books

Library of Congress Cataloging-in-Publication Data
Names: Kirby, David, 1944– author.
Title: More than this : poems / David Kirby.
Description: Baton Rouge : Louisiana State University Press, 2019.
Identifiers: LCCN 2019001729 | ISBN 978-0-8071-6985-8 (cloth : alk. paper) | ISBN 978-0-8071-6986-5 (pbk. : alk. paper) | ISBN 978-0-8071-7207-0 (pdf) | ISBN 978-0-8071-7206-3 (epub)
Classification: LCC PS3561.I66 A6 2020 | DDC 811/.54—dc23
LC record available at https://lccn.loc.gov/2019001729

The paper in this book meets the guidelines for permanence and durability of the Committee on Production Guidelines for Book Longevity of the Council on Library Resources. ♾

If I can't dance to it, it's not my revolution.

—EMMA GOLDMAN

I like beautiful melodies telling me terrible things.

—TOM WAITS

Play it fuckin' loud!

—BOB DYLAN

CONTENTS

xi *Acknowledgments*

I. BILL AND I GO TO CHRISTINE McINTIRE'S CHURCH

3 What the Great Poets Say about Love
5 Look, Slavs
7 The Doors of Perception
10 Your Decision Will Be a Hard One
12 I Love You, John Maynard Keynes
14 Bill and I Go to Christine McIntire's Church
16 Big Meal with Gioachino Rossini
20 How'd We Get This Far
22 Uncanny
24 I'm Gonna Stomp Your Guts Out
26 The Things I Can't Tell You

II. ALWAYS SOMETHING THERE TO REMIND ME

31 Just Beyond the Fence, a Train
36 Poverty, Mon Amour
39 Tony Bennett Sings "Smile" for You
43 Not Easy to Believe

44 So Far, So Good
46 Love Me Tender
48 The New Jerusalem
50 Poking Stuff with Sticks
51 You Found That Thing You Lost
52 This Living Hand
54 Always Something There to Remind Me

III. SATISFACTION

57 To an Athlete Dying Young
59 1973
61 Grumpy Old Woman
63 We Three Kings
66 I Have Not Come Here to Compare Notes but to Sit Together in the Stillness at the Edge of This Wound
67 Frida Loves Diego
69 Satisfaction
72 King of Good Fellows
75 Pictures at an Exhibition
78 The Rhetorical Device Known as What-Aboutery
81 I Can

IV. MARY WEISS OF THE SHANGRI-LAS EXPLAINS IT ALL TO YOU

85 Dear Chestnuts, French Babies, Statues, and Bees
88 If You Were John Riley
91 All Art Is the Blues
94 Space Dogs
96 What to Call It
99 My Lousy Saint

101 The Chronicle of Higher Education
103 Ode to Ignorance
105 Mary Weiss of the Shangri-Las Explains It All to You
107 More Than This
109 A World in Which These Things Happen

111 *Notes*

ACKNOWLEDGMENTS

I am grateful to the editors of the print magazines and websites where these poems first appeared, occasionally in different versions: *The Account*: "Big Meal with Gioachino Rossini" and "My Lousy Saint"; *American Journal of Poetry*: "Frida Loves Diego"; *American Poetry Review*: "I Can" and "Tony Bennett Sings 'Smile' for You"; *Baltimore Review*: "I Love You, John Maynard Keynes"; *Birmingham Poetry Review*: "Poverty, Mon Amour"; *The Boiler*: "You Found That Thing You Lost"; *Ducts*: "Grumpy Old Woman," "I'm Gonna Stomp Your Guts Out," "To an Athlete Dying Young," and "What the Great Poets Say about Love"; *Ecotone*: "Satisfaction"; *Five Points*: "Poking Stuff with Sticks"; *Gulf Coast*: "The Things I Can't Tell You"; *Howl*: "King of Good Fellows"; *New Orleans Review*: "Ode to Ignorance"; *The North* (UK): "Dear Chestnuts, French Babies, Statues, and Bees" and "Your Decision Will Be a Hard One"; *One*: "The Chronicle of Higher Education"; *Oxford American*: "1973"; *The Pinch*: "Love Me Tender" and "The Rhetorical Device Known as What-Aboutery"; *Plume*: "If You Were John Riley"; *Prairie Schooner*: "The New Jerusalem"; *Rattle*: "Mary Weiss of the Shangri-Las Explains It All to You," "More Than This," and "This Living Hand"; *Shenandoah*: "Look, Slavs"; *Smartish Pace*: "A World in Which These Things Happen"; *Southern Review*: "All Art Is the Blues" and "How'd We Get This Far"; *Spillway*: "Uncanny"; *Split Lip*: "Bill and I Go to Christine McIntire's Church"; *Terminus*: "Pictures at an Exhibition," "We Three Kings," and "What to Call It"; *Valley Voice*: "Space Dogs"; *Waxwing*: "So Far, So Good"; *Willow Springs*: "Not Easy to Believe."

"Always Something There to Remind Me" appeared on the Best American Poetry blog, and "I Have Not Come Here to Compare Notes but to Sit Together in the Stillness at the Edge of This Wound" was featured on the Academy of American Poets' Poem-a-Day site. "More Than This" was selected for inclusion in *Pushcart Prize XLI.*

Thanks also to the Florida Humanities Council for a residency at the Hermitage Artist Retreat, during which time I finished this book. Additional thanks are offered in the notes section at the end.

I

BILL AND I GO TO CHRISTINE McINTIRE'S CHURCH

WHAT THE GREAT POETS SAY ABOUT LOVE

"I would my love could kill thee," says Swinburne in "Anactoria."
I wonder what he meant by that. I could find out if I actually
read the poem, but it's well over 300 lines. I like short poems,
don't you? Also, what's with the "thee"? Scholars think
"Anactoria" may have been written in 1863, by which

time I'm pretty sure people were saying "you" when they were
referring to the person standing in front of them, or at least
Walt Whitman did. Whitman! Now there's somebody who
knew a lot about love, probably because he didn't seem
to have much in his life—well, the cosmic mystical double

whammy woo-woo juju kind, yeah, but not the kissy
cuddly kind. For that, you have to go to, I don't know,
Allen Ginsberg, who lived in a day when you could talk about
that kind of thing more freely. Actually, the poet who
may have known the most about love is George Herbert,

who tells us that "quick-eyed Love" beckoned him, yet he
drew back because he felt himself so unkind, so ungrateful
that he wasn't worthy to even look upon Love, who tells him,
"Who made the eyes but I?" and he keeps protesting,
and finally Love tells him to sit and "taste my meat,"

and he says, "So I did sit and eat." Thing is, when you
love somebody, you really do want to kill them
or at least you want to pull their flesh off in handfuls
and stuff it down your gullet, but only if you could
do that and still have them appear before you unharmed

once you've had a chance to rest up and get ready
to devour them again. That's the thing that's baffling
about love, that makes us come back to it again and again
like a dragon with all the fires in the world in its heart,
but hidden, because you don't want to scare her, scare yourself.

LOOK, SLAVS

Remember when you were a little kid and somebody said
"Slav" and you thought they said "slob" and wondered
if the two words were the same and then realized they weren't
but thought they might be connected in some way and that
maybe Slavs are messy and throw their underpants on the floor

and leave their dishes in the sink or are said to do those things
by their sworn enemies, the Whomevers, the people who live
across the river, on the other side of the valley, in the heart
of the dark wood. What are Slavs, anyway? Answer:
an Indo-European ethno-linguistic group, even though members

of that group are diverse both genetically and culturally and relations
between them vary, ranging from a sense of connection to mutual
feelings of hostility. Slavs have even waged war on other Slavs.
Why, though? Listen up, you Slavs: your ancestors spoke
the same languages you do and shared cultural traits and historical

backgrounds—why can't you get along? I know, it's because
of what Freud called the narcissism of small differences,
or "the need to distinguish oneself by minute shadings and to insist,
with outsized militancy, on the importance of those shadings."
But Marie Curie was a Slav, and so were Tolstoy and Tchaikovsky.

Why not bond in pride over these illustrious predecessors?
Even better, in the sixteenth century, the bodyguard of the Doge
of Venice consisted largely of Slavs, which makes sense:
if your bodyguards were Venetians, some of them
might belong to families that hold a grudge against yours,

and you know what that would lead to: gossip, rumor, betrayal,
stabbings, people trying to trip you as you cross the Rialto,
somebody else saying, "Look out the window!"
and dumping a white powder into your wine glass,
and when you turn around and say, "I didn't see anything—

say, what's this white powder in my wine glass?" they'd say, "Oh,
that? I don't know. It's white powder. Drink it! It's good for you."
But a Slav wouldn't do that. They'd be on the payroll.
They like it that you're the Doge, and they want you
to be the Doge for as long as you can. I wish I were a Slav.

No, wait—I don't. I want to be the Doge, with Slavs
on every side. Slavs to protect me, to get me from one place
to the next, to keep me focused on the business of the Republic,
to put others above myself and insure that Venice is a safe
and happy place brimming with culture and enterprise, with

green industries and vigorous bilateral trade agreements
but also musicians in every piazza and only the finest plays in our many
Venetian theaters. I love my bodyguards. Every time I look
into their honest Slav faces, I think, "I'm the Doge." Only Slavs
can save us. Only people who aren't us can tell us who we are.

THE DOORS OF PERCEPTION

Between every two pines is a door leading to a new life.
—JOHN MUIR

You couldn't be more right about that, John Muir.
Actually, a door leading to a new life can be
found between two anything; it's just that we're liable
to find it faster in nature, not that many of us are
in nature all that much these days. Instead,
we're inside, where there are more electrical outlets.

And more doors, though these are all little doors,
whereas what we want is what nature writer
Stephen Graham calls the great door: "As you sit
on the hillside," says Graham, "or lie prone under
the trees of the forest, or sprawl wet-legged
by a mountain stream, the great door, that does not look

like a door, opens." *That does not look like a door.*
Hmm. . . . My experience with doors that do not
look like doors is largely if not entirely literary, as when
I dip into the great Finnish epic the *Kalevala,*
where the hero Väinämöinen is trying to
build an enchanted ship but needs three magic words

to finish the job. So he looks for them "in the brains
of countless swallows": no luck. Same
with "the heads of dying swans," "the plumage
of the grey duck," "the tongues of summer reindeer,"
"the mouths of squirrels." So he does what you
or I would do and sets out for the Deathland of Tuoni,

where he almost succumbs to an evil enchantment
but escapes and is sitting dazed on a hillside,
where he meets a shepherd who tells him
he has to enter the underworld and find the deity
Wipunen, so off goes Väinämöinen to Wipunen's
burial place, a cleft in the hillside, and Wipunen

opens his immense mouth, which just happens
to be the cleft in the hillside, and in goes
Väinämöinen, and out he pops after three days,
saying, "I have learnt a thousand magic words,
and among them are the three I sought."
Good stuff, right? Few among us are epic heroes,

of course, so it's just as well that, insofar as they
function as portals to new and fantastic worlds,
doors are just as available to little kids as they are
to gigantic hairy-legged axe wielders
like Väinämöinen: yet a third great nature
writer, Robert Macfarlane, picks up this idea when

he says, "To young children, of course, nature
is full of doors—is nothing but doors, really—
and they swing open at every step." For example,
"A hollow tree is the gateway to a castle."
Funny: all these great nature writers, and all
they can think of is doors. Maybe we see doors

in field and forest because there aren't any, and
since we'd rather be home in the first place,
we invent them. Well, there you have it.

And even though I am not a nature writer,
I, too, have talked myself into a preference
for metaphorical doors, such as, for example,

the lover's mouth, for who, upon putting his or her
two lips to the lips of his or her beloved,
does not feel as though a door has just opened
to a world outside of space and time, one occupied
by the two paramours alone? As in the Song
of Solomon: "Let him kiss me with the kisses

of his mouth," says the speaker in that poem,
"for thy love is better than wine," and then
"a bundle of myrrh is my well-beloved unto me,
he shall lie all night betwixt my breasts."
When I kissed Barbara the first time
I thought, umm, tasty! but also yeah, new life.

YOUR DECISION WILL BE A HARD ONE

When a teenager is caught smoking pot on a street corner
or decides to borrow his friend's mom's car without asking
the mom and wrecks it or doesn't turn in any homework

for an entire semester even though he or she actually
completed that homework and brought it to school every day
but somehow never got around to turning it in, and you yell

at that teenager, *What were you thinking!* the correct answer is,
I wasn't! though of course your teenager will say *Okay,*
it happened, but not the way you think or *Everybody else*

is doing it, why can't I? or *I don't know, it's not my fault,*
it's somebody else's fault, it's yours. Regardless of age,
you have more control over these things than you think:

when Linda Ronstadt hears Emmylou Harris sing
for the first time, she is eaten up with jealousy, but then
she realizes that jealousy will keep her from ever hearing

Emmylou's beautiful voice again, so she decides to
eighty-six those feelings of envy, to chuck, dump, jettison
them, tell them to amscray. As the Chinese proverb says,

you cannot prevent the dark birds of sorrow from passing
over your head, but you can keep them from nesting in your
hair. Okay, I know it's a proverb; I thought it was Chinese.

If you're lucky, your decision will be a hard one,
as it was for the student who asks his advisor whether
he should major in psychology or art history, to which

the professor replies, "Is this a hard choice for you?"
and when the student says yes, the professor says,
"In that case, it doesn't matter. If it's a hard decision,

then there's a lot to be said on both sides, so either choice
will be good. Hard decisions are unimportant." When
I was young, I played in a garage band. Nobody listened

to us but us. We did not play softly. We were no good.
The Clash song "Garageland" says, "I just wanna stay
in the garage all night." It might have been written for us.

I LOVE YOU, JOHN MAYNARD KEYNES

"Every point on the earth," said 13th-century Franciscan
        friar Roger Bacon, "is the apex of a pyramid filled with
the fires of heaven." I wonder what he meant by that.
                Probably that there's all this power under our feet and that
        it's up to us to figure out how to unlock it, which, for you

writers, means to write as though your life depends on it,
        because it does. Put yourself in Dante's shoes: in the Seventh
Circle of hell, there's a river of boiling blood and a forest
                of souls that become suffering trees, not to mention centaurs,
        including Nessus, who fires off a couple of arrows but then

gives Dante and Virgil a ride out of there on his back.
        You can't make this shit up, folks. You have to be there, see it,
write it all down. Otherwise, you're just turning
                the Magic 8 Ball over and over: "Most likely," "Outlook
        doubtful," "Try again later," "My reply is no." That's why

top-shelf British economist John Maynard Keynes said that
        "words ought to be a little wild, for they are the assaults
of thoughts on the unthinking." Actually, I like the Magic 8
                Ball and use it often to make decisions which aren't very
        important, which, let's face it, most decisions aren't.

Should I eat at Wo Fat's or Waffle House tonight?
        "Concentrate and ask again." Do I need to take a shower
or just paw myself with a washrag? "Better not tell
                you now." John Maynard Keynes, I love you so much
        I want to call you John Maynard the way Southerners

call people Sue Ellen and Billy Joe. You're so much
smarter than the Magic 8 Ball. But words shouldn't
be wild all the time, John Maynard! What if words
were wild all the time? Either we'd be overwhelmed,
like people slathered in whipped cream, then given

hot-chocolate enemas and wrapped in live electrical
wires before being tossed into tubs of stale chablis mixed
with rancid mayonnaise, or else our senses
would become so dull that, instead of jumping around
like somebody wearing a jacket made of mice

and a pair of cheese pants who's standing under
a molasses shower as pygmies with blowguns shoot darts
tipped with sneezing powder at him, we wouldn't react
at all, and the words wouldn't be wild any more:
"dynamite" would be no more powerful than "filtered tap water,"

"ecstasy" the same as "nap." You writers make these
little buildings of mud and diamonds that most readers
will never even notice, much less enter the way Wilbur,
the neighbor's cat, waits on our deck till I let him in,
saunters through every room in the house as though

he's thinking about buying it, and then walks right
past me without even looking as he leaves, as though to say
"No catnip farm, tuna pond, milk river?" In addition to
John Maynard Keynes, I also love Keats, silent upon his peak
in Darien and thinking about his next poem, thinking hard.

BILL AND I GO TO CHRISTINE McINTIRE'S CHURCH

High school seniors, we go to a different church
each Sunday, wanting there to be a God so we can

doubt Him. The Quakers are calm, the Methodists jovial.
At the AME church, the pastor recognizes the sisters

of the Omega Sapphire sorority in their big hats and then us,
"our very special guests," everyone turning to look

at the white boys. One Saturday we go to the synagogue
and are fed bagels and lox afterward, though we don't

know which are the bagels and which the lox.
Then there's Christine McIntire's church. Christine

is the most beautiful girl in our class. She's more
excited about our project than we are, and when we ask her

what kind of church hers is, she says, "Just come."
The people in Christine McIntire's church begin

with a prayer, but in minutes they're screaming
and throwing themselves around the room and tearing

their clothes. They're stormy petrels, these people.
They're going to Graceland. A man runs through hell

in a gasoline sport coat. A woman scrambles across
the trunk of the death car like Jackie Kennedy trying

to retrieve the back of her husband's head.
The people in Christine McIntire's church drive trucks

for a living and stamp out sheet metal and sweat
long days in those chemical plants by the river

that are killing them slowly. They're homesick for a place
they've never been. They're what Bill and I want to be,

passionate about what matters to them and, after that,
indifferent. They're in love, these people, they're all shook up.

BIG MEAL WITH GIOACHINO ROSSINI

I tell my students not to use words like Beauty and Truth
because, first, nobody will know what you mean and, second,
nobody cares—they'd much rather go on a picnic with somebody
and try to make out with them or roast a chicken or have

their oil changed and tires rotated than sit around and worry about
whether or not such actions are beautiful or true. Yet when I am
in Florence, whereas most people hurry to the tomb of Michelangelo
in the church of Santa Croce or gather in front of the monument

to Galileo there, I always bend a knee before the sepulcher
of Gioachino Rossini and think, beauty! Where would we be
without *The Barber of Seville* and *William Tell*? Why, there'd
hardly be any popular culture at all, no Daffy Duck or Tom

and Jerry cartoons or *Lone Ranger*, all thanks to this jolly
fat man who composed so beautifully. Or jolly-seeming,
I should say: who knows what joy lurks in a man's heart,
fat or not, and the same goes for the heart of a woman,

though to comment on a woman's size is something no man
would ever do, or at least no gentleman. As for truth,
there are two ways to look at it. Think of that James Bond movie
in which James Bond is trapped in a hall of mirrors and thus

faced with multiple images of the villain, so that it is only
when he shatters all the mirrors that he sees his enemy
in the flesh, suggesting that we, too, are surrounded by distractions
which we must eliminate in order to get at the truth,

which is imminently get-at-able. Then there is the school
that says no, truth is a rabbit in a briar patch, that when
you reach in and try to seize it by the neck, you put your hand
on the spot where it used to or will be but isn't. So which

metaphor do you like, the hall of mirrors one or the rabbit
in the briar patch? Wrong question, since it assumes that truth
can only be expressed in words, whereas the truth that springs
from your music is no less true for being inarticulatable

any more than a beautiful dinner is less so for being anything
other than itself. Gioachino Rossini, how I would love to sit down
to table with you. Let's start with some antipasti misti,
then on to the pasta course: ravioli filled with ricotta and spinach

for you, and for me, fettucine with ragù. Now for the hard part,
which is fish or meat? Okay, meat: we'll have fish next time.
One of us should get the veal chop and the other the veal cutlet.
It doesn't matter to me, either; let's just get both and decide

when the plates arrive, though we're also going to need some
side dishes, a plate of fried zucchini flowers, maybe, and artichokes
sauteed with garlic and parsley. Okay, and now to the essential:
what shall we drink? Brunello, Barolo, Barbaresco, Nebbiolo,

Sagrantino—why, the very names sound like your lyrics!
You like Haydn, don't you? Of course you like Haydn, probably
for the same reason Keats did. Keats said that Haydn was like
a child, "for there is no knowing what he will do next."

May we not say the same of your Figaro? "Everyone asks for me,
everyone wants me," Figaro sings, "women, children,
old people, young ones," and no wonder: "I am the luckiest,
it's the truth! Ready for anything, / night and day / I'm always

on the move." That's the way, isn't it? Moving from one thing
to another, no matter how big or small the thing, how long
or short the journey. Look, the antipasti! Often you were left
in the care of your aging grandmother, who had difficulty

supervising you, so while your father played his horn
and your mother sang, you were left in the care of a butcher
and later apprenticed to a blacksmith—no wonder you're
at home in the heart of the ordinary people, of a barber, say,

or a serving girl. This chop is bigger than that cutlet,
and I want you to have it. No, no, I insist. I'm putting
my foot down, Rossini! Pass the vegetables, please.
"One can't judge Wagner's opera *Lohengrin* after

a first hearing," you say, "and I certainly don't intend
to hear it a second time." Ha, ha! Strong passions, Gioachino,
strong passions! You say, "Give me a laundry list,
and I'll set it to music." How about a cheese course?

Oh, that's right: you're the one who says ice cream, always.
Sempre gelato: if every politician had that as his or her
campaign slogan, they'd all get elected, and then where
would we be? And if you can make a sonata or a cantata

or an étude or a scherzo out of a laundry list,
think what you could do with this beautiful dinner
we're having! I'm glad the restaurant is playing Bellini
and Donizetti tonight. I bet you'd feel silly if we were

listening to your *Lady of the Lake* or *Cinderella,*
though I want to say that when I listen
to those works on my own, I feel I'm in touch with something
that's bigger than this world, that's infinite, even,

that dishes up more love than I've ever encountered
anywhere, more compassion, excitement,
gentleness, more grace and virtue of every kind.
Music doesn't teach us anything. It teaches us everything.

Yes, yes, it's late, but do let's take a digestivo,
a grappa or Sambuca or both. It can't hurt—
well, it can, but who cares?
Tomorrow we'll wake up with information and sore heads.

HOW'D WE GET THIS FAR

is what old people say when they're talking to other old people
about how stupid they were when they were young, not realizing
that it's young people's job to be stupid, to ride skateboards
and fall in love with people they just met and pound shots and drafts
until they can't remember their own names and then wake up
the next day to a breakfast of Twizzlers and Mountain Dew before

going off to class. Late. How boring it would be to live in a world
where 20-year-olds peddled down the street on those adult tricycles
and married people who'd undergone a rigorous vetting process
and consumed no stimulant stronger than filtered tap water
and green tea. When I was in grad school, my mates and I
dropped acid and, in the fullness of our pharmaceutically enhanced

certainty that we were at one with the universe, decided to pile into
a couple of cars and set out for the woods, there to feel the force
that through the green fuse drives the flower and speak with the birds,
only when the driver of the first car had the presence of mind to stop
at a stop sign that the driver of the second car failed to notice,
that vehicle, which included yours truly, collided with the other,

removing its bumper and causing the heads of its occupants
to bounce off one another, not to mention the windows, wheel,
dashboard. That same year, I'd been called into my advisor's office.
The rule was that, at any time during a student's first year,
he or she could be dismissed simply for being thought not to be
a good fit with the program, and since one of my roommates

had already been let go in this manner, I saw myself as next.
The call from the departmental secretary came on a Friday afternoon,
and since I couldn't see my advisor till Monday, by the time

I walked through his door, I was ready to rake everything off
his desk and tell him what he could do with his stupid program,
though it turned out that his favorite niece was coming into town

from Charleston for the regatta, and he and his wife decided that
the perfect escort would be the nice Southern boy, that is, me, who
knew to hand cups of punch to the ladies first and make conversation on
a variety of topics instead of devouring all the sandwiches himself
and complaining about his professors and all the theoretical crap
he had to read. Good thing I didn't rake everything

off his desk. Susan Sontag says interpretation is the revenge
of the intellect upon the world; it impoverishes and depletes it,
and, indeed, my certainty that I was about to be dismissed
almost resulted in an action that would have made my dismissal
certain, though happily some older and wiser voice in my head
called out from the future and directed my still young and stupid

self to pause for a moment before hurling into the air my advisor's
desk pad, calendar, coffee cup, half-corrected proof of one or more
scholarly articles, pen set, eyeglasses, framed photo of favorite niece.
How do we know, though. After the one car smashed into the other
during our dope-fueled trip to the country, we continued on for a couple
of miles and parked beside a stream and some picnic tables

and got out, and the driver of the second car said to the occupants
of the first, each of whom by now was gazing at the flowers
in wonder or caressing the bark of a tree, "Dude, dude, sorry
about that wreck," and a fellow who was in the process of removing
his clothes, to what end I either never learned or don't remember,
looked up wild-eyed and said, "What wreck?"

UNCANNY

Who did you think you saw just now at the bank,
the grocery store, in the park? Was it your father,
your teacher, your lover, all dead? Psychologists
say the uncanny means something that's not just
mysterious but somehow strangely familiar, as in
Susan Cooper's *The Dark Is Rising,* where a boy

wakes to strange music which rises loudly
and then fades, and when it does, the world
he knows goes with it: no roofs or lawns
or fields outside his window but a great forest,
covered in snow, and while these changes
scare the boy, they don't surprise him,

because they were already there in his mind,
though he didn't know it, already within
his sense of the possible. One minute
we're laughing with our loved ones
or just talking quietly, and then they die,
and we're in a world that's not this world,

one in fragments and without light, a world
like one of Piranesi's imaginary prisons, all
engine and machine, all wheel, cable, pulley,
lever, catapult, and you the tiny figure climbing
a staircase that appears to lead to an exit,
though it doubles back and becomes itself again,

over and over, a place you know because
you've been here before, but only briefly
and in dreams, though this time you see

your way out, so you walk up to the man
in the fedora and overcoat who's at the counter
filling out a deposit slip and say *Dad, is that you?*

Or you tap the shoulder of the woman handing
the cashier a bag of plums and some cheese
and say *Mrs. Parham, you taught me*
to do long division—remember?
You were so patient with me, with us all.
It's enough to make you think the dead

haven't left entirely or have come back,
not so they could see us, but so we can see them,
can edge closer, put out a hand to touch them,
which is why you make your way through
the people in the park to the woman you just
saw—it's your first real girlfriend, you think,

the one who taught you that the way to make
a woman happy is to listen to her and be gentle,
and she's feeding the pigeons now or just standing
quietly by the pond, watching the children
playing with the little toy sailboats, and you say
Excuse me, excuse me until you get to her

and touch her shoulder, and you say *Jane, Jane,*
I still have a lock of your hair and she turns,
and her hair is white now, but her eyes are still
as blue as cornflowers, and she looks at you
quizzically for a moment and then smiles, and you
can't say which is brighter, the sun or her face.

I'M GONNA STOMP YOUR GUTS OUT

After the wedding, I play I'm Gonna Stomp Your Guts Out! with
half a dozen amped-up kids, which is easy: all you
have to do is shout, "I'm gonna stomp your guts out!" and then
the other players shout, "I'm gonna stomp your guts out!"
and then you growl and make a face and start
stomping everybody's guts out. What fun! Everybody knows

exactly what to do. In a 1986 study at the University of Pennsylvania,
students were asked to put labels reading "sucrose"
and "sodium cyanide (poison)" on two identical bowls
of sugar, and even though the students could put either
label on either bowl, once they'd labeled them,
they were reluctant to sweeten their coffee or tea with sugar

from the one that they'd just labeled poison. Silly students!
I would have done the same, though. Who knows whether
something might have happened in the interim to alter
the chemical composition of the two substances,
even though that interim would have been less
than the time it took you to read this line. Salman Rushdie

says there is something lost in translation but something
gained as well. Fun, for example: when my student
Nick Sturm tells me that sometimes he thinks
of William Carlos Williams as Tom Waits and T. S. Eliot
as the Eagles, I laugh so hard I almost wet my
pants. To equate Dr. Williams with the Grammy Award–winnng

singer/songwriter whose voice, according to one critic,
sounds as though it was "soaked in a vat of bourbon,
left hanging in the smokehouse for a few months,

and then taken outside and run over with a car" is a
great stroke, but to turn that brilliantined
stick-insect Eliot into both Don Henley and Glenn Frey

as well as all the other Eagles is nothing less than a signal day
for American humor, also literary criticism. I myself
take on different names from time to time, imagining,
for example, that my first name is that of Arcangelo Corelli
as I finish my exercises and make a protein shake
while listening to that worthy's Concerto Grosso Opus 6

No. 4. Archangel! Who among us would not be
a prodigy were not this his or her name, the fact
notwithstanding that there have been no doubt
many mediocre, not to mention downright incompetent,
Arcangelos in the history of our glorious if not
always totally stellar race. Still, may one not be Arcangelo at

one moment and oneself at another, just as Winnie the Pooh's boat
is sometimes a Boat and sometimes more of an Accident,
as he says, depending on whether he is on top of
or underneath it? Why, to go through life as oneself
seems like a kind of imprisonment imposed upon
temporarily inconvenienced noblemen or bosomy gypsy girls

by a cruel despot in a medieval fable or allegory of some kind,
although in this case, the cruel despot who imposes
the terrible punishment would be you. After twenty minutes or so
of playing I'm Gonna Stomp Your Guts Out! the kids run off
to get more soda and cupcakes, but one little girl comes
back and says, "I was just playing." "I know," I say. "I was, too."

THE THINGS I CAN'T TELL YOU

Alex and Catherine's dog Seamus is old, fat, and blind; he looks
like a cocktail wienie with four toothpicks for legs,

and Alex and Catherine are trying to help him find me so he can
bite me, but Seamus keeps bumping into chairs

and running into walls, so I get down and pat the floor and say,
"Over here, Seamus! Over here! I'm so scared!

You can bite me! I'm ready! Over here!" though by the time he
finds me, his anger has been exhausted and he's all

wriggly and licky. But isn't that the way it always is? Something
is itself, and then it becomes another thing

entirely. After Woodrow Wilson loses his beloved first wife
to Bright's disease, he sinks into a deep depression

from which he emerges only after meeting 43-year-old Edith Galt,
a widow herself and someone who is drawn

to the president but doesn't want to be the president's wife—
who would? Also, the *Lusitania* has just been sunk,

and hawks were clamoring for war with Germany. Finally Edith
relents, though, and off they go on their

honeymoon in a private railcar to Hot Springs, Virginia,
enjoying a late supper of chicken salad.

The next morning, Secret Service man Edmund Starling looks
into the railcar's sitting room and sees "a figure

in top hat, tailcoat, and gray morning trousers, standing with his back
to me, hands in his pockets, happily dancing

a jig." Even better, the president, still oblivious to Starling's presence,
clicks his heels in the air and sings,

"Oh, you beautiful doll! / You great big beautiful doll!" A dog
wants to bite us and then changes his mind.

A president can barely drag himself out of bed in the morning,
and the next thing you know,

he's dancing to a ragtime tune. And yet . . . *Io no mori'*
e non rimasi vivo, said Dante

when he saw Satan frozen in ice at the bottom of Hell:
"I did not die and I did not remain alive."

Between the thing and its opposite, there may be sights we can't
unsee yet are unable to name: You read that

the dead of the *Lusitania* were often seen in "humiliating" positions,
and it isn't till later you find out that many

of them had put their life jackets on upside down and so
drowned that way, their legs in the air

like figures in a Bosch painting. And one survivor reported
seeing a woman give birth in the water.

II

ALWAYS SOMETHING THERE TO REMIND ME

JUST BEYOND THE FENCE, A TRAIN

I'm running down the Via dei Serragli on the way
 to the Missionaries of Mary house before it closes
when I notice that the gate to the Torrigiani Gardens
 is open, and since I've been trying to get through

that gate for years to see the tower where the ghost
 first appears to the governess in Henry James's
Turn of the Screw, I dart through it before
 the custodian tells me to get lost the way he's done

a half dozen times earlier, and sure enough, there's
 that tower, which James moves to England for his story,
its square base representing the earth, in the words of
 the architect, the octagonal middle "the conjunction

between the earth and the astral level," and the round top
 "perfect knowledge." Of what, though? The Jews
in Florence thought they were safe in 1943, but after
 the roundup and deportation of 1,022 Roman Jews

to Auschwitz, the Nazis quickly go north to make
 surprise raids in other cities. The young chief rabbi
of Florence asks the archdiocese to shelter Jewish
 refugees in convents and monasteries, and the Missionary

Sisters of Mary in Piazza del Carmine answer the call,
 taking in eighty Jewish mothers and their children,
though at 3:00 a.m. on the morning of November 27,
 they wake to the sound of soldiers breaking through

the iron gate. In James's story, too, things proceed
slowly until they don't: a nameless young governess
is hired to care for two children, Flora and Miles,
on a remote country estate, the only other inhabitant

of which is Mrs. Grose, the housekeeper. Then
the governess sees a menacing figure on the tower
one evening who reappears outside the dining room
window, as though looking for someone. The man

has "red hair," she tells Mrs. Grose, "very red,
close-curling, and a pale face, long in shape,
with straight, good features and little, rather queer
whiskers that are as red as his hair." Mrs. Grose

falters and then says the governess has described
Peter Quint, a former servant, and Peter Quint is dead.
One nun rings the alarm bell when the German soldiers
break into the Missionary House, but where can

the women go? "*Aufstehen!*" the soldiers shout
as they go from room to room,"Get up!" They take
the women and children to the auditorium, where
where one soldier checks each name on a list, another

interrogates them, two more take their money and jewelry.
A girl named Lea Lowenwirth-Reuveni tries to escape
by jumping from a window but is caught and brought back,
and when the Germans learn she speaks several languages,

they make her the interpreter, and Lea persuades them
        to release many of the women, convincing their captors
that they are undocumented Hungarians. The governess,
        too, wants to save the children from Peter Quint,

but then another ghost appears, that of Miss Jessel,
        her predecessor, and soon after, the governess sees
Peter Quint inside the house, on the staircase; he looks
        at her and turns slowly and descends, and a month later,

she sees Miss Jessel inside the house as well, "dishonored
        and tragic . . . dark as midnight in her black dress,"
in "her haggard beauty and her unutterable woe."
        It's at this point in the story you realize that, in Virginia

Woolf's words, Henry James has conquered, because
        if you've turned off the light, you'll wake and turn it on
again an hour later, for "that courtly, worldly, sentimental
        old gentleman can still make us afraid of the dark."

That's when you say to yourself, yes, the ghosts are real,
        I believe in them or else I wouldn't be turning
this light on. There's a problem, though, which is that
        the only person who has seen the ghosts is the one

who is telling you this story. The Germans begin
        to shove the women Lea Lowenwirth-Reuveni couldn't
save out the door and into trucks that will take them
        to a prison in Florence and then Verona and the camps

at Auschwitz-Birkenau, from which none return.
In the confusion, a woman drops her son Isaac
at a nun's feet, and the nun steps forward, hiding the baby
under her skirts; today that child is a father and lives

with his family in Israel. Except for that part, the true story
is too horrible to believe. And we don't know what
to make of the invented one: in James's final paragraphs,
the governess is alone in the house with Miles

when the ghost of Peter Quint appears one last time
outside the window. Miles utters "the cry of a creature
hurled over an abyss," the governess says, but "I caught him,
yes, I held him—it may be imagined with what a passion;

but at the end of a minute I began to feel what it truly
was that I held. We were alone with the quiet day,
and his little heart, dispossessed, had stopped."
We are so dazzled by money and power, says Primo Levi,

that we forget how fragile we are, forget that we are in
the ghetto, all of us, and around the ghetto is a fence,
and beyond the fence stand the lords of death,
and beyond them, a train waits, a curl of steam

from its boiler disappearing into an indifferent sky.
If there's no such thing as ghosts, the governess must have
been insane. But if you thought dead people were trying
to get into your house, what would you do? Lea

Lowenwirth-Reuveni tried to run away, but when they
caught her and she realized she could save others' lives, she did.
The baby lived because a nun took one step forward.
You can't save everyone. You save whom you can.

POVERTY, MON AMOUR

Editor asks me to write a piece on the music scene
in Augusta, Georgia, so I head up there and do what
I always do, which is just start talking to the first person
I see, and sooner or later I hook up with a fellow named
Rick Stanley who is, shall we say, something of a character,

which comes as no surprise seeing as how he became Elvis's
stepbrother when his divorced mom married Vernon Presley,
and Rick says, *I had a rough time growing up—I didn't get*
my first Cadillac till I was 13 and then pauses to see
if I get the joke, which I do, though I'm not in a laughing

mood at the moment because I'm thinking about my friend's
wife who has just died and who, of all the wives, was
the most beautiful, and not just in a physical way, though there
was that, but because she knew how not to call attention
to her beauty and to use it instead with her warmth

and intelligence to set any room ablaze just by walking into it,
and the other husbands envied him right up to the moment that
he woke two mornings ago and found she wasn't breathing.
Thing is, it's so easy to die: *Mr. President, you certainly*
can't say that Dallas doesn't love you, Nellie Connally

says to John F. Kennedy, and Jackie smiles and turns
and is watching his face as the bullet hits. *He looked puzzled,*
she says later. *He looked as if he just had a slight headache.*
And then, as if in slow motion, his head begins to come apart.
The president still has a faint pulse when he is admitted

to Parkland Hospital, and as the doctors work on him,
                they ask her to leave, *but it's my husband,* she says, *his blood,*
his brains, are all over me. She's still wearing that pink Chanel
                suit, and *she refused to take it off,* a friend will say, *as though*
she didn't want the day to end. Jackie's Catholic, educated:

will she remember her Dante, how, when he gets to
                Paradise, he meets Thomas Aquinas, who begins to tell him
about Francis of Assisi and how the saint fell in love with
                a woman and how they had children together? Now Dante
was known for his temper, and you can imagine him barking

in anger at these words, so Aquinas hurries the story along
                and says the woman was a widow, that she lost her husband
eleven hundred years earlier, that she lived her life *slighted*
                and obscure and without a single suitor till Francis came along,
and now the two are so fond of each other that *their concord and glad*

looks, wonder and love, / And sweet regard gave birth to holy
                thoughts, and the lady's name is Poverty. Poverty: we forgot
about her, didn't we? We were too busy with the house, the car,
                the job. The doctors at Parkland watch as Jackie kisses
her husband's foot, which sticks out from beneath the sheet

they had covered him with, and then she pulls back the sheet,
                uncovers his face and shoulders, and begins kissing him again,
starting with the foot and then, through the sheet, slowly
                working her way up, kisses his leg, thigh, chest, lips, thinking
goodbye, Jack, goodbye, my treasure, my riches, money,

mint, mine. There's a service for my friend's wife when
                    I get back from Augusta, a celebration, really, with music
and photos and people telling stories to remind us yet again
                    how lovely she was and how she changed everyone around
her for the better, especially her children and her husband,

and when I talk to him, and he says, *Your accomplishments*
                    mean nothing, David. It's just you and Barbara, and just then
somebody comes up, and the two of them start talking,
                    which is good, probably, because when someone says
something like that to you, you're speechless, or at least I am.

Pretty much the last thing Rick Stanley says to me before
                    I drive back from Augusta to start writing that piece about
the music scene there is, *Son, when Elvis died, how much*
                    money do you reckon he left behind? and I'm trying
to guess, but before I can say anything, he says, *All of it.*

TONY BENNETT SINGS "SMILE" FOR YOU

Tony Bennett is 90! And we love him because, like all
successful entertainers, he conveys that sense
of loving us as well, and he also loves his material—
indeed, before he begins his next number, he says,

"I really love this song. Its composer lived in Switzerland,
and when it became a hit, he wrote me a note,"
and we think, Switzerland? because we can count the number
of famous Swiss songwriters on the fingers of one hand,

and not even that. What's Switzerland famous for? Okay,
the cuckoo clock, as Joseph Cotten famously points out
in *The Third Man*, also cheese and neutrality. Of these,
surely the most important is neutrality, especially when

one's neighbors include the Germany where Hitler comes
to power in 1933, which is also the year when a woman
named Francine Christophe is born. Eleven years later,
she is deported to the Bergen-Belsen concentration camp

along with her mother. They survive somehow, and the adult
Francine Christophe recalls that the deportees are allowed
to bring a few personal items into the camp, so her mother
packs away two small pieces of chocolate, knowing that

her daughter will need them some day when she collapses
from hunger, though when a pregnant woman named Hélène
goes into labor, the mother asks Francine Christophe
if she can give the chocolate to Hélène instead, saying

it may save her life, and Francine Christophe says,
        "Yeah, sure, I'm fine," and the mother gives Hélène
the chocolate, and Hélène gives birth to a baby girl,
        and the baby girl survives, and six months later, the camp

is liberated. The composer of the song Tony Bennett
        is about to sing is, of course, Switzerland's most famous
non-Swiss citizen, Charlie Chaplin. "Dear Tony,"
        he'd written, "thank you so much for resurrecting my song

and making it famous all over again." "And I couldn't
        believe the signature," says Tony Bennett. "It was signed,
'Mr. Charlie Chaplin,'" who used the tune as a theme
        for his 1936 movie *Modern Times*. "Smile, what's the use

of crying," sings Tony Bennett; "you'll find that life
        is still worthwhile, if you just smile." Francine Christophe
grows up and marries and has her own children, and one day
        her daughter asks her if she thought that the deportees

would have been better off after returning home in 1945
        had they had access to psychologists or psychiatrists,
and Francine Christophe replies, "Yeah, sure, but we didn't
        have them." Now imagine that you're Francine Christophe.

You're in your eighties now. And you can't stop thinking
        about the question your daughter asked, so you decide
to have a conference to discuss these issues of trauma
        and resilience and survival, and you invite Holocaust survivors

as well as therapists and mental health professionals of every
kind. In *Modern Times,* Chaplin plays an assembly-line worker
driven mad by the monotony of his job, and for the rest
of the film, he can't catch a break: he's in and out

of the asylum, in and out of work, in and out of jail,
and along the way, he meets an orphan called simply
the Gamine, played by Paulette Goddard, and he keeps
taking on new jobs so he can be her friend and protector,

but every job ends with a dismissal and another jail term,
and when orphanage officials show up to claim the Gamine,
she moans, "What's the use of trying," but Chaplin tells her
to never say die, and the film's last image is of the two

of them strolling down a California highway towards
new adventures. At the conference, Francine Christophe
recounts the horrors that she and her mother underwent:
"I'm frightened, Mother," you say. "Last year, I was seven

years old. This year, I'm eight, and so many years separate
these two ages. I have learned that I am Jewish,
that I am a monster, and that I must hide myself."
And then the experts begin to read their papers, and when

one of the speakers approaches the podium, she begins
by saying, "I live in Marseille, where I am a psychiatrist."
And she says, "But before I deliver my talk, I have something
for Francine Christophe." And she takes a piece of chocolate

from her pocket, and she hands it to you, and you think, what
in the world? And the audience sees this coming, and they're
in tears, but by now you're smiling at her, and she says,
"I'm the baby," and she smiles at you, and you smile.

NOT EASY TO BELIEVE

My brother's colleague is on trial for murder. He had a pulley
in his bedroom that he used to lower his wife out the window

in the hours before dawn, and then he'd go outside and have sex
with her, though my brother never got the details on that.

One morning, the rope breaks, and the next thing he knows,
my brother's colleague is in jail. He says it was consensual,

that his wife asked for it that way, but the state says he killed her,
that it was a deliberate act, he wanted her dead. "All truths

are easy to understand once they are discovered," says Galileo;
"the point is to discover them." Once I was having a drink with

a friend, and he told me that his marriage was over, that he
and his wife barely spoke to each other, and then his wife

joined us and began to talk about the trips they had planned
and the vacation home they were thinking of buying.

If we knew what we liked, why would we ever do anything?
Many thought Bobby Fischer the greatest chess player of all time,

but when asked if he enjoyed himself after a visit to a brothel
in Curaçao, he said, "Chess is better." In the end,

my brother's colleague got off. The defense had a witness.
It was the paperboy; he'd peddled by many times on his route,

saw them loving each other, said of the two, the wife took
the most pleasure, filling the darkness with her silent cries.

SO FAR, SO GOOD

The prisoners in a German work camp near Hanover got used
to the indifference and cruelty of the guards who gave them

watery soup and worked them nearly to death and were therefore
all the more heartened by the behavior of a stray dog that had

somehow gotten into the camp and who greeted the prisoners
as they returned exhausted from the forest where they spent

their days chopping wood, barking with joy and flinging himself
about as dogs do. Maybe the men enjoyed the dog's silliness.

Maybe the dog reminded the men that the shadow of war
would pass sooner or later, that there were things beyond its reach.

In the camp at Ravensbrück, doctors performed experiments
on female prisoners to test the effect of sulfa drugs on battlefield

injuries. Healthy limbs were amputated, muscle and tissue removed
without anesthesia, and then the women were put against a wall

and shot. Before they were executed, the women pinched
their cheeks to put color in them and did each other's hair.

I ask a woman at a party what they wanted, and she says,
"To be fully human for as long as they could, for every second

of the lives that remained to them." Elie Wiesel says that
"the opposite of love is not hate, it's indifference. The opposite

of beauty is not ugliness, it's indifference. The opposite of faith
is not heresy, it's indifference." Maybe the women, too, knew

the artillery would fall silent one day, the troops go home.
It's not a matter of being pretty or feeling good about yourself.

It's a matter of not going to your death with your hair in your face.
The guards offered them a sedative, but not all the women took it.

LOVE ME TENDER

A student tells me the old Greeks identified seven types
of love—eros, philia, storge, agape, ludus, pragma,
and philautia—to which I reply *Well, I'll be damned*
because we're just standing around in the hall after class,
though later I think there's the kind of love you have
for Grandma Beverly and then the kind you have for your

baby doll, but who knew there were five more? And to think
that I learned this from a student, I, a professor and graybeard,
even though I have no beard, and if I did, I'd shave it off
if it were gray, because who wants to look older than he already
is these days. But seven! This makes me wonder what type
of love is being described in the story I read in the newspaper

about the man whose young wife died unexpectedly,
and as he waits in the hospital for her organ donor surgery,
family and friends keep coming in to say their goodbyes,
and the surgery is now an hour away, and he's exhausted,
and all he wants is to be alone with her one last time,
and he starts to fall asleep in the recliner by her bedside,

which is when the two nurses, Donna and Jen, say *We have
an idea,* and they ask him to leave the room for a minute,
and when he comes back in, he sees that Donna and Jen
have moved his wife to the right side of her bed, leaving him
just enough room to lie down with her and nestle his body
into hers and tell her *You look so beautiful* and stroke

her hair and face and pull down the top of her gown
and kiss her breasts and then lay his head on her chest, feel it
rise and fall, her heartbeat in his ear. Your first thought

is how wonderful Donna and Jen are and your second
and deeper thought is what a wonderful husband and wife
and what a loving and intimate marriage theirs was,

and then you think, but what did he know about her, really.
Aren't all marriages like the one in the fairy tale about
the blacksmith who stops at an inn in this one town
and sees a woman coming out of the house across the street,
a beautiful, pale woman in an elegant dress with a ribbon around
her throat, and he begins to court her anyway and wins her

over and proposes, and she agrees to marry him, but under one
condition: he can't ever ask her to remove the ribbon. *Of course,*
says the blacksmith, and they're very happy together, though
he can't stop thinking about the ribbon, and she reminds him
of his promise, but he can't sleep, and at last one night she says
Is this what you want? Do you want me to remove the ribbon?

and he says *Yes,* and she unties the ribbon, and her head falls off.
Well, they tried, didn't they? Maybe love is not a thing with
seven names at all but simply something we do the best way
we can, and about this time I realize that I have not heard
from my friend Natalie for some time and wonder if I've
offended her, so I write her and say *I've been thinking*

about you, Natalie, and weeks go by, and finally I think
Well, I guess that's it for me and Natalie, but it isn't, because
the next thing I know, Natalie's writing back full
of good cheer and saying *Well, well!* and *How are you?*
and then *You're thinking about me because I'm always*
watching you and from a bright window in my heart.

THE NEW JERUSALEM

The mother and father turn the map over, confused,
while their daughter checks her phone, so I say

This is my campus, let me help you, and after I tell
them how to find the admissions office, the father says

What will Patricia learn at your university,
and I say We will teach her that beauty is something

she can recognize and master, that it's on a scale
we understand and in this way differs from

the sublime, which is mysterious, even terrifying,
and he turns to his wife and says Did you hear that,

honey? I knew we'd picked the right school.
And the mother comes over and says Once she

learns this, will the Holy City come down from
heaven like a bride beautifully dressed for her husband?

And I tell her No, that won't happen until she learns
that you ought not distinguish where you cannot divide,

yet you must divide, or you will never grasp the whole.
The mother fingers a tube of lip balm and says

And that will be the New Jerusalem, when God
makes his dwelling place among the people?

And he will dwell with them, and they will be
his people, and God himself will be with them,

with our Patricia and the others? And I say Yes,
yes, that's right, only they won't know he's here.

POKING STUFF WITH STICKS

It's what I did between six and fourteen. Sure, school
figured in somewhere, and I read a lot, mainly at night,
but girls hadn't arrived on the scene, and I wasn't that great
at sports or music, so I'd go out into the woods and poke stuff,
sometimes in the company of other boys, most often by myself.
I don't remember the stuff or the sticks, but I do remember
the poking, and the poker, which was me. Someone said
the separation between the hand and the hammer disappears
in the act of hammering. Also between the hammer and the nail,
also between the hammer and the thumb of your other hand
when you miss the nail and hit your thumb instead.
But I didn't think about that then. I was like both the Irish monk
who wrote the poem about his cat and the cat as well,
the one trying to trap the best words, the other, mice.
"In our arts we find our bliss," says the monk, "I have mine
and he has his." Neither art is easy. Someone else
said that whereas a good poet sees the difficulty in the poem,
a great poet makes the difficulty part of the poem.
I think that was Paul Valéry; he seems to have said every smart
thing that wasn't said by someone else. I opened the door
just now, and it wasn't my yard at all but the woods
I played in as a boy. So much stuff out there, just waiting.

YOU FOUND THAT THING YOU LOST

The planner with all your dates in it, your ring, even something
of no importance at all: your favorite pen, say, though you can
buy a dozen at the corner drugstore, or the list of things you
want to do today, even though you remember writing nothing
more than "call George" and "buy coffee." You didn't need
to do that: you'll know to buy coffee when you run out.
And which George? You know three Georges. If you can't
remember which one to call, maybe you don't need to call
any of them. What do you need? If you were a doomsday prepper,
it would make sense to have beer and wine. It would make
more sense to have a book that told you how to make beer
and wine, and, by the same token, if not guns, at least friends
with guns. Penicillin, bleach, solar panels: you'd need all that,
and an acoustical instrument so you could while away the hours.
Paranoia, self-righteousness. . . . Oh, and a copy of *Ulysses*—
you'll be able to get through it this time. Comic books,
board games, chewing tobacco, a fishing line and hooks,
duct tape, aluminum foil, Vaseline: all that less one thing,
the one you want to lose. There's something you'll regret
bringing with you into your cave, that should have stayed
outside on the treeless earth with its ceaseless winds
and that light that never changes. What is it?

THIS LIVING HAND

Tom Mannarino defends his MFA thesis brilliantly, but when
I stick my head in his office door to say so, he's slumped
in his chair and staring at the floor, and when he looks up,
there's no other way to describe him than horror-struck.
Tom's thesis is a novel about his escape from a crushing

religion and the freedom he finds in the love of men, and now
that it's written and we're all telling him it's brilliant,
he realizes that he's at a turning point, that his story isn't
academic any more, that it will be published and people
will see it, his family included. It's so hard to connect

with others sometimes. Keats wanted to: Leigh Hunt remembered
that his young friend looked often at his hand when he was
near death, a hand "faded and swollen in the veins, and say
it was the hand of a man of fifty," and then Keats turned
from one of those long poems he was no good at to write

in the margin a fragment that begins "This living hand,
now warm and capable" and ends "see, here it is" and
"I hold it towards you." In Celtic theology it's said that heaven
and earth are only three feet apart, but there are thin places
where the distance is even smaller: "The door between this world

And the next is cracked open for a moment," wrote one mystic,
"And the light is not all on the other side." When soldiers
at the Battle of Little Bighorn realized the jig was up, they shook
hands with one another. Goodbye, Calhoun! Goodbye, Ross.
And the Arikara scouts kissed their horses and told them they loved

them. Tom, you try to live your life, but home calls you back.
On a beautiful May morning, your parents are away.
You mow the lawn, put the mower back in the garage,
pick up the gas can, pour its contents over you,
strike a match. Tom, it should be a better world. It isn't.

Why didn't you just leave? Two hundred years ago in Philadelphia,
wise men wrote, "We hold these truths to be self-evident:
that all men are created equal." Why couldn't you believe them?
Jefferson had originally written "we hold these truths to be
sacred and undeniable," but Franklin struck the three words

that made the claim religious, changing it to a claim based
on reason instead. Tom, you weren't thinking, were you?
Maybe religion could have saved you, though not
the kind that says people who are different from us are evil.
Paul McCartney was fourteen when his mother died of cancer.

Later, she came to him in a dream: "It was great to visit with her again,"
he said, and then he wrote "Let It Be" because in the dream,
his mother told him, "It will be all right, just let it be." Keats' hand
was faded and swollen, but his skin is clear now, his fever cooled.
Can you see? It's just here, Tom. He's holding it out to you. Take it.

ALWAYS SOMETHING THERE TO REMIND ME

It's 1992. Bosnia tries to break away from Yugoslavia, and its capital city,
Sarajevo, is surrounded by Serbian soldiers who kill nearly 12,000 people,

though not this one teenager, a journalist now, who lived communally
in a basement with other youngsters. The boys would go off to fight

and then return to the girls, who lived there full-time. They slept together
on mattresses on the floor and ate together and fell in and out of love,

as young people do, and talked about literature and told jokes and,
since some of them had brought instruments, staged their own concerts.

I wonder what they played. When I was their age, so many songs
had utopian titles: "Share the Land," "Get Together," "People Got

to Be Free." What were you thinking, Grass Roots, Youngbloods,
Young Rascals? Later I wondered if we were that stupid,

and then I thought, no, we just wanted hope, wanted to stop our war,
let everyone vote, get a cup of coffee at any lunch counter, anywhere.

When the teenager was wounded in a bombing, her parents
smuggled her into Italy to recuperate, but she was so unhappy there

she had herself smuggled back to Sarajevo, which was even harder
than leaving it. Their war ended. Today new buildings dot the city's skyline,

and there are even tourists. The girl and her friends grew up, got jobs,
started families. Life got better, though not in the way they thought.

III

SATISFACTION

TO AN ATHLETE DYING YOUNG

Three tall young women all but trample me as I walk
across campus, so vigorously are they horsing about—
punching each other, whooping, receiving greetings
from passersby and returning same—and I think,
volleyball players, and then, how glorious to be
a top athlete, to give your body directions and have it
obey instantly or just after, should the situation call for it,
as when the forward fake-pumps the ball to confuse
his or her opponent and only then flips it through
the net. Or when, the fullback crosses the goal line, say,
though not before gesturing with his head toward
the snack stand, as though to suggest to his would-be
tackler, "I hear it's two-for-one quesadillas today—
how about I treat you?" Housman wrote of these things.
In the poem for which my own poem is named, he writes,
"The time you won your town the race / We chaired you
through the market-place; / Man and boy stood cheering by,
And home we brought you shoulder-high." Later,
the same people bear the runner through the streets again,
only dead this time. Housman seems to think that's
a good idea: "Smart lad," he says, "to slip betimes away
From fields where glory does not stay." And maybe
it'd be better not to become famous; then you wouldn't
have to worry about dying on time. Last week, a student
read a poem asking whether you'd rather watch
your parents have sex every day for a year or participate
with them just once, and someone else asks if suicide
could be a third option, and the student says no,
because everybody would choose suicide. One person
says she'd jump right in and get it over with, but another
says no, then you'd suffer forever from PTSD, and yet

another student says, yeah, Parental Trisexual Stress Disorder. Don't die, athletes! Don't die, anybody. Oh, go ahead: it's not as though you have a whole lot of choice in the matter. Circus performer Mario "The Human Cannonball" Zacchini said that flying isn't the hard part, landing in the net is. Fly, athletes! We all land in the net. Not everybody flies.

1973

Kid comes to see me during my office hours, and he says he had
a weekend job at a gas station, and one Saturday, two girls
from French class come by and ask him if he wants to go
skinny-dipping, and he says, Yeah, sure, but he has to work
till seven, so the girls take off down the highway to the sinkhole,

which is when the kid turns to the black guy he works with
and says, I've got to find another job, and his coworker says,
Hmm, I think I know a fellow you can talk to, so when he gets
off work, the kid drives down to this barbecue shack
in Wakulla County and goes around back and knocks on the door,

and this huge man opens it and looks left and right and then down
at the kid, and says, What you want, fella? and the kid says,
I hear you need a helper, and the big man smiles and says,
I been thinking about hiring me a white boy, and the next thing
he knows, the kid has an apron around his waist and he's stirring up

a batch of barbecue sauce in a bathtub with a mop—not
the same mop he uses at night to swab the floor of the tiny
dining room before he locks up and goes home, but a barbecue
mop. I never did find out what happened to the girls.
I bet there were other girls, though. "If you but knew the flames

that burn in me which I attempt to beat down with my reason,"
said Pushkin. Another student tells me she went out
with a guy once in high school, and he spends the night grabbing
her breasts, and she spends the night fighting him off,
and she goes to college, and she goes to grad school,

and one day she's playing kickball with her classmates
and passes out in the Florida heat, and her classmates
call an ambulance, and when she wakes up, an EMT
is unbuttoning her blouse so he can attach electrodes,
and she starts screaming because the EMT is the guy

from high school. He isn't pawing her breasts, though.
Not this time. This time, he wants only to save her.
Whenever I eat barbecue, I think of the kid who
worked at the gas station and the two girls
in their shorts and bikini tops who stop for just

a moment at that gas station and then ride out of his life forever.
I never did find out what happened to the kid, either.
Still, I'm happy for him. He learned how to want things,
how to change your life in order to get them,
how you always get something else instead.

GRUMPY OLD WOMAN

Florence. Or Rome—really, anywhere in Italy

She's everywhere in this city: I see her behind a cash register,
ironing some guy's shirt in a doorway, sweeping the courtyard.
She's grumpy already, and if I say "*Buon giorno!*" to her,
she'll look up, scowl, turn grumpier still. I blame her husband,
who was probably mean to her while he was alive and then
did her the disservice of dying before he could mend his ways
or she could take her revenge. Or it could be her children,

the ungrateful parasites. Who wants to get pregnant? I know,
plenty of women, but just as many don't, yet they meet some
careless fellow, and there you have it. How I love the angels
in the great paintings who tell Mary she is with child, some
as pushy as door-to-door salesmen and others contorting their
bodies like wrestlers, trying to get under the guard of a woman
who just wants to sit in her garden, read her book, nibble

her apricots, and drink her tea without taking on the problems
of the whole fucking world. And if Mary looks mildly pissed,
there are plenty of other women who are out of their minds
with rage: look at the Judith in Artemisia Gentileschi's painting,
cutting off the head of Holofernes—girl's sawing
away as her maidservant caresses the tyrant as though
he'd just had a mani-pedi and were settling down for

a shampoo and a light trim. Judith's mad about something—
mad about everything, probably. And who can blame her?
For centuries the church fathers have been telling women
they're temptresses, they're bad just for walking down

the street, for looking pretty, for smiling, for saying hello
and also for not saying hello because either way they make
men mad, make them do things they wouldn't do otherwise,

women are horrible, they're everything that's wrong
with this world, don't blame me, I didn't do it, they did,
it's their fault. Men, we can do better. Men, look into the face
of your grumpy old woman. Novelist Ursula K. Le Guin
tells that the tired old faces we see in paintings delight us
because they show beauty that is not skin-deep but life-deep,
and if that is true for a work of art, how much truer must

it be for your Luisa, your Francesca, your Gemma, Gina,
Beatrice. You were Adam once, and she Eve, and there
was a garden, and a snake, sure, but there's always a snake,
and here's the road that leads from that garden to this world,
which isn't worse, really, just different, and you have to
work now, but there's something about work that satisfies you
deeply: you're making things that people want, and if

your boss is a little stern, he smiles at you from time
to time, and you sense that he sees something in you
that you don't even see in yourself, and you like
Tommaso and Michele, the guys you work with, and nobody
liked Andrea, but he's gone now, and if the hours are long,
the pay is good, and when you come home, there she is,
and you have your whole lives ahead of you.

WE THREE KINGS

Two students are arguing in the library, the one saying,
"You are your résumé," and the other saying, "I'm not
my résumé!" and the other saying, "Yes, you are."
I agree with the first student more than the second:
if you rob banks and liquor stores and break into people's
houses and steal from them while they're sleeping,

chances are you're a crook, whereas if you give food
to the hungry and medicine to the sick and bathe the sores
of lepers and make sure orphans have a bed to sleep in
and enough to eat, you're probably Mother Teresa.
Are you your name, though? Many of us have the same
ones. Same name, different person: Aretha

Franklin gave us Aretha Franklin, whereas Bertha Franklin
shot Sam Cooke to death in a seedy LA motel, even though
he kind of had it coming—the first Franklin gave us one
of the greatest soul voices ever, the other took one away.
Then there's Martin Luther King, Jr., B. B. King,
and lead singer Ben E. King of the Drifters,

two more musical legends and the father of the civil
rights movement, a saint, really, though deeply human,
as saints always are. During the Renaissance, some
painters thought it was disrespectful to paint Jesus
as a little boy and tried to make him look like the Jesus
everybody knows, the one who preached sermons

on love and mercy and not a baby who squalled
when he was hungry or needed his diaper changed
and otherwise lolled around on his mother's lap

with his finger in his mouth and looked at the cat,
the dog, the moo-cow, which, as the dictionary
tells us, is "a child's name for a cow." Yet is not

"moo-cow" as good as and, in many ways, superior
to "mature female domesticated ungulate"? Like
the Lee Harvey Oswald who shot JFK, the man
who shot Dr. King had three first names, as though
the midwife stuttered as she called him first "James"
and then "Earl" and finally "Ray" before

she threw up her hands in disgust and gave him
to the devil. The two vehicles outside the Lorraine
Motel are a '59 Dodge Royal with massive,
olive-green tail fins and a white '68 Cadillac
as big as a rail car on the right. Dr. King and his friends
were going to dinner in them

that April evening, and the cars have been there
ever since. Swing low, sweet chariot, coming for
to carry me home. What would Jesus or Dr. King
have given the world had they lived into their middle
years and beyond? During World War I, Private Henry
Tandey of the 5th Duke of Wellington Regiment

watches the German troops in retreat and raises
his weapon as a wounded soldier enters his line of fire
and says later, "I took aim but couldn't shoot
a wounded man, so I let him go," thus sparing the life
of 29-year-old Lance Corporal Adolf Hitler, who nods
in thanks and limps off into the future. Each of us

is who we are, is the person he or she is at the moment
in which he or she is him or her and not the person he
or she was just before or will be just after.
Poet Mary Ruefle reminds us that the greatest thing about
our greatest playwright is that "in the beginning
William Shakespeare was a baby, and knew

absolutely nothing. He couldn't even speak." Yet out
of that baby comes *King Lear,* and out of other babies
come the Declaration of Independence, the formula
for Prozac, the business plan for Facebook.
Nothing argues the supreme importance of names
to human civilization; everything argues

the supreme importance of humans to civilization.
Who named you, anyway? Who cares.
Let Gaspar, Balthasar, and Melchior be the wise men.
Let Moe, Larry, and Curly be the wise guys.
Let the baby be the baby. If he's lucky, he'll be
a king some day. One day, we'll all be.

I HAVE NOT COME HERE TO COMPARE NOTES BUT TO SIT TOGETHER IN THE STILLNESS AT THE EDGE OF THIS WOUND

Asked if it isn't weird to be at an awards ceremony with Gregory Peck,
Dylan says, "Well, listen, everything's weird. You tell me something

that's not weird." He might as well have said "big," that his songs are
a witness to magnitude, that your poems are. And why shouldn't they be?

Look at the epic of your life, at the people in it, all heroic. And to think
it began with an accident. Somebody looked up at the night sky and saw a star,

somebody in Cracow or Belgrade, maybe, or the city where you live now.
Carbon, nitrogen . . . there was an explosion, and now you have to pay attention

to everything. At the party, everyone was talking about the crappy TV series
that's so popular, and you didn't say you wanted better, wanted more.

That same night, you met the man you'd love so hard it made your teeth hurt.
He said, "Hey, baby," and you snapped, "I'm not your baby."

I have nothing to say to you, really. I just want to see what I'm looking at.
I want so much not to listen to you after all this time but to hear.

FRIDA LOVES DIEGO

"He does it very gently, in the French way," says the woman
across the table, and when I look up and smile, she says,
"I was talking about opening oysters." Okay, but still.
Frida Kahlo says "you deserve a lover who goes to paradise
every time he looks into your eyes," one who brings you "hope,

coffee, and poetry." She would say that, wouldn't she, since
her lover was that big fat slob Diego Rivera, the foremost
muralist of his time yet not what anyone would call great
husband material. And what a waistband! In some photos,
tiny Frida is embracing big Diego, her little head resting

on his enormous stomach. Ha, ha! He looks like an elephant!
And she like the little cat who is the elephant's best friend
in some of your more popular pet videos. Yet he had
something going for him. Frida met Diego in 1927
when she was an art student, and soon their relationship

became intimate. Their marriage was tumultuous.
Both had multiple affairs. Frida had affairs with both men
and women, though Diego only had affairs with women.
Some people would give him points for that, except
that one of the women was Frida Kahlo's younger sister Cristina,

which, as her biographer says, "infuriated Kahlo."
Frida says "you deserve a lover who makes you feel safe,
who can consume this world whole if he walks hand in hand
with you," one who "believes that his embraces are
a perfect match with your skin." But notice she says

"deserve" over and over again, and "you": so "you deserve"
rather than "I have." Frida and Diego divorced in 1939
but remarried a year later. Although their second marriage
was as troubled as the first, they remained married till
her death in 1954. Diego was more famous in their lifetimes,

though Frida is thought of as the better artist today.
The French way of opening oysters means leaving
some brine in the shell so you can taste the sea.
When we taste our true loves, does not the whole earth enter
our mouths: sea, forest, library, sky? What we deserve

and what we have aren't always the same thing.
Between what we have and what we deserve is the space
where we paint our paintings, build our buildings,
write our poems. Between what we have and what we deserve
is what we never wanted in the first place but is better.

SATISFACTION

Barbara says, "Don't let me forget to be happy about such-and-so":
poem accepted, headstand in the middle of the room instead of against

the wall, big-thumbs-up teaching evaluation, note from a long-lost friend.
This is the same Barbara who snuggles up behind me at night as I say,

"Ummm," which is when she says, "How do you know it's me and not
the clown who lives under the bed?" and I scream so loudly I wake

the neighbors, who deserve to be woken, the shits, since they're the ones
who lopped a twenty-foot branch off our two hundred-year-old

oak tree, though of course I am more delighted than scared to have
such a fun wife. Why is it so hard for us to be happy? I know, because

life stinks. Lear says to Cordelia, "Stay a little," but it's too late:
he's speaking to her lifeless body, and he's already lost his mind.

There's no joy like that of a kid, of course. One thing I've learned
from riding around the park near my house is that if there's a kid

on a bicycle and you point and say, "I'll race you to that lamppost,"
every one of them will hunch over their handlebars and start pedaling

as though their little lives depended on it. Then there's young man's
love, all jizz and ardor. When Apollo chases Daphne and she turns

into a tree, he still loves her, and when he places his hand against
the trunk, he feels her heart beating beneath the bark and embraces

the branches as if they were limbs and kisses the wood, though
even as a tree, she shrinks from those kisses. Apollo should have

cooled his jets, n'est-ce pas? It says right here in the *New York Times*
that "no matter how much in love you are at 20, there's a whole

new definition of love that awaits you at 65, and if you knew what
it was when you were 20, you'd spend your life being impatient,"

and if the *Times* doesn't know, who does? After all, it's the newspaper
of record. Time does make you see things differently: can you imagine

how Niccolò Polo felt when he saw Venice after 17 years in the court
of the Great Kublai? All that time he'd been with people who were nice,

sure, but they didn't look like him, talk like him, eat the food he ate,
and now he's in the Piazza San Marco again, having a drink

with friends, buying a cone of roasted nuts, turning to look at a woman
who may have been his lover once and is fat now and missing a tooth

but still beautiful. And sometimes we're sad when we thought
we'd be happy: heavyweight champ Rocky Marciano cried after

he defeated the aging Joe Louis because he was glad he'd won,
but he knew he'd beaten an old man. No wonder we need someone

to remind us to be happy, such as German poet, philosopher, historian,
and playwright Friedrich Schiller, author of the "Ode to Joy" best known

for providing the final movement of Beethoven's Ninth Symphony
and whose words address Joy, that daughter of Elysium whose shrine

we enter fire-drunk because her magic binds again what custom's sword
had parted, making beggars brothers to princes! Joy drives the wheels

in the great clock of worlds, says Schiller, lures flowers from their buds,
suns from the firmament! Joy rolls spheres in the spaces that the seer's

telescope does not know, she bubbles in the cup whence even cannibals
drink gentleness! Fly from your perches, brothers, when that cup is passed,

and let the foam spray to the heavens—uh-oh, Schiller's sounding
like Apollo there, isn't he, reader? Yet joy abounds. There's no end to it.

"All rivers flow into the sea," says Ecclesiastes, "yet the sea is not full,"
though we complain again and again that it is. "Can't get no satisfaction,"

says Mick Jagger, though there is no greater satisfaction than a well-made
song—well-made anything, really. Oh, and someone to like it.

KING OF GOOD FELLOWS

Emerson says a reader can nestle into Plato's brain
but not Shakespeare's, yet what is Shakespeare
doing if not throwing everything against the wall and seeing
what sticks? He just piles one image on top of the other
like a father showering presents on his children,
the gifts arriving so quickly that all experiences are devoured,

all categories broken down, all distinctions annihilated,
and we see the world as it really is, a mishmash, a glorious shiny
mess where I am king and you are queen, though neither of us
wears a crown. Otherwise, why bother? Why write at all
if you're not giving away the store, tossing out your shiniest
presents, bestowing your best boons, favors, benefactions?

As good Sir Thomas Browne says, what songs the Sirens sang
are not beyond *all* conjecture. Why, we might even come up
with better songs than the ones they actually sang. To limit
oneself is to tempt the fate of Sancho Panza's kinsmen, the one
tasting a hogshead of wine and saying he found
in it a taste of leather, and the other doing the same, only finding

instead a hint of iron, and so both were ridiculed and made
to feel a failure, though when the hogshead was drained,
what was found at the bottom? That's right: a rusty key
with a leather thong. Don't limit yourself, poets! Do you
think Shakespeare said "I better limit myself" just
before he writes Act 2, Scene 1 of *Midsummer Night's Dream,*

where Oberon tells Puck how he sat on a cliff and saw
a mermaid riding on a dolphin's back and singing such
a song as made the very world bend a knee to its beauty

and then saw as well Cupid flying between the earth
and the moon and firing an arrow at a Vestal
virgin and missing her, though the arrow lands on a white flower

and turns it "purple with love's wound," and this is
the very flower that Puck will now fetch to bewitch fairy
and high-born Athenian alike and spark such japes, jibes,
shenanigans, tomfoolery, and star-crossed love as have
ne'er been seen this side of the Peloponnesian Peninsula,
and there you have it: Shakespeare could have had Oberon

say, "Fetch me that flower," as indeed he eventually does,
but he also gives us a mermaid, a dolphin, a song so sweet
as to calm the sea and shake the very stars, not to mention
Cupid, a virgin, a flower made magic by the god's arrow,
and all told by a sorcerer to his apprentice
because Shakespeare is so generous, so kind to us, his audience,

so possessed of a mind that makes no distinction
between anything and anything else, be that thing
literary, philosophical, musical, military, historical,
gastronomic, genealogical, geographic, or jurisprudential,
and by offering us such rings, toys, conceits,
knacks, trifles, nosegays, KitKat bars, and other messengers of strong

prevailment as these does he invite you and me
to play a game, really, an elaborate game that's totally
realistic and, at the same time, make-believe, like a dream,
one that the eye of man has not heard, the ear of man
has not seen, that man's hand is not able to taste,
his tongue to conceive, nor his heart to report what it is, in other words,

a dream no one has dreamed yet, but you're in it, and you're
the star, and though you tore across the stage in the very torrent,
tempest, and whirlwind of your passion, you spoke your speech
so trippingly that it acquired and begat a temperance that gave it
smoothness, and you weren't too tame, no, you let your own
discretion be your tutor and suited the action to the word,

the word to the action. And the other players: aren't
they good? Plus they're just fun to be with even when
you're not on stage. But you are now, and our play
is done, and you're all laughing and bowing as applause
crashes down on your heads—let lightning spit fire,
let rain spray! And you smile and nod

as you look this way and that, and when you turn
to the player on your left, it's Shakespeare himself,
and he has a role, too, a minor one, as usual, and you say,
"Shakespeare!" and he says, "Your honor," and you say,
"Thank you for writing this," and maybe it's the applause
or your own giddiness or the girl who plays Hermia

that you've been wanting to ask out on a date, and not
the let's-all-go-to-a-movie-and-hang-out kind of date
but a real date with just two people, and she's looking
at you now as though she has never seen one so fair,
but anyway, and this is the best part, you can't
help believing Shakespeare when he says, "I didn't write it, you did."

PICTURES AT AN EXHIBITION

They look alike at first, your fellow art lovers, and then you begin
    to see distinct groups: the ladies who appear
to be young from the back, for example, but when
    they turn around, you realize they're not. Eat a sandwich,
ladies! Leave celery to the rabbits. And go shopping,
    will you? All the knee boots, fringed shawls, and silver

concho belts in the world aren't going to make anyone think you're
    twenty-five again. As for you over-forty
guys with ponytails, get a haircut! Don't you know
    that, at your age, a man with long hair looks like
an old frontier woman? "Hand me that there rifle,
    Paw, there's renegades on the warpath!" I don't know

who the average over-forty gal pretending to be twenty-five
    is looking for, but I bet it's not an old
frontier woman. Then there are the people in wheelchairs.
    God love them! There are two kinds of people in this world,
the ones in wheelchairs and the ones who aren't
    in wheelchairs yet, and you folk scooting around

just under eye level and rolling over my feet and bumping
    my shins are just preparing the rest of us.
Not for you cable TV with its steady diet of dangerous
    sports, vapid reality shows, commercials for products
that are only sold on TV because no one in his
    right mind would buy one in a store, and newscasters

who have long since consigned to oblivion the past perfect,
    that indispensable construction that tells us
one action has finished before another starts—no, sir!

Here you are among the Van Goghs and the Gauguins
and the Berthe Morisots and the Puvis de Chavannes—
you go to museums so often you probably even know

how to pronounce Puvis de Chavannes, for which I respect you
even more, since no one else does.
And you kids. You're so lucky! The fathers of Paul
Cézanne and Camille Pissarro tried to keep them
from becoming artists, whereas your dads are pushing
you through the museum in strollers and dropping down

on one knee to explain that, in the words of sculptor François
Rude, sculpture is "a plate and chestnuts,"
that is, flat planes but three-dimensional volumes
as well. Then there are the guards, many of whom
are men. The male guards offer helpful comments
if you ask for them, though I notice they offer these

same comments voluntarily to pretty young women. Older
women, if you want the attention of the male
guards, why not ask them what pointillism is or whether
the "t" at the end of Seurat is silent or not. You'll sound
smart, and we men love smart women, though it appears
otherwise. As for the rest of us, a sign says that Cézanne

is "widely considered the father of modern art." Where does
that leave you and me? We're not the father
of anything except ourselves. And even that's complicated:
commenting on his sculpture *Theseus and the Minotaur,*
in which Theseus is depicted killing the minotaur,
Jacques Lipchitz says, "I realized that the monster

is also part of Theseus, as though there were a Hitler in each
        of us whom we must destroy," and then,
"Theseus is killing part of himself." If I were
        a museum guard, I wouldn't speak to the pretty young
women at all so as not to appear creepy. It's not
        that I'm creepy, though if I were, I'd try to kill off

that part of myself the way Theseus kills the minotaur. Actually,
        I'm on the minotaur's side, just as I always
cheer for the bull instead of the matador. Where would
        we be without plates *and* chestnuts? Where would we be
without the multiform, the multifold, the multifarious?
        Where would museums be if every picture were the same.

THE RHETORICAL DEVICE KNOWN AS WHAT-ABOUTERY

I'm smiling at the waitress who botched my order:
the owner is angry at her, and she's about to cry.
She's like a Poetic Technique student,
that is, a student in the class that precedes Poetry Workshop
and where one learns the carpentry
of poetry, so to speak, the measuring, sawing, hammering,

and fitting of one piece to another until the whole
is finished and the gaps between the different pieces
are not as glaring as they might be, and as
I think of this and continue to smile at the incompetent
waitress so she'll feel better about
her job and get back to work and become a competent one,

I also think of the rhetorical device known as
what-aboutery, which is when you say, "You drink
too much" to someone, and they say,
"Oh, yeah? What about Jasmine next door? She always puts
out her trash cans at night and wakes
everybody up," and you say, "What does that have to do with

your drinking problem?" and the other person
says, "Shut up!" and you say, "No, you shut up!"
and you have a lively if ultimately pointless
exchange for fifteen minutes or so, all because your idiot friend
or nephew or brother-in-law uttered
a little two-word phrase that acted as a kind of booster rocket

and lifted your conversation to a funner level, the point
being that it takes a while to get from where
you are to where you want to be, especially

if you don't know where you're going in the first place,
    which you shouldn't, for, as the scientists
say, if you know what you're doing, it isn't research.

    And this is the what-aboutery of the poem, which is
its biggest part, if not necessarily its most important.
    Both waitresses and Poetic Technique students
are like the man in the Gospel of Matthew who finds a treasure
    in a field and buries it again and sells all
he has and buys the field and the treasure into the bargain,

    which is pretty much the American Dream, or
the Galilean Dream, considering that the man who
    finds the treasure is a penniless peasant
who has managed to make a killing and also put one over
    on a master who no doubt not only beat
his laborer but also told him more than once that he was not nearly

    as astute in the ways of the world as he, the master, was.
So let's say you've amassed all this treasure,
    all these incandescent images, these lovely
words and phrases as well as any number that are deliberately
    unlovely because often the homely word
or phrase is exactly what's needed in this wonderful poem of yours

    that you haven't actually written yet because now
you need to house all that language "in structures
    that are a delight in themselves," according
to the great Jack Gilbert, that is, the lines and stanzas
    that will ensure your deathless poem's
deathlessness. Above and beyond all that, though, and this

is the hard part, now you've got to come up with
that little thing that charges all this gorgeous
what-aboutery of yours with electricty,
that strikes as surely as that fire from the heavens that struck
the neck bolt of Victor von Frankenstein's
monster and made him jump up off that table and do

the Pony, the Twist, the Watusi, the Mashed Potato.
Speaking of food, the restaurant owner calms down
after a few minutes, so the waitress
cheers up and brings me what I ordered in the first place,
which are these little *polpettine* or meatballs
that are so good that I ask the waitress what the secret is,

but the restaurant owner, though calm now, is still
hovering over her to make sure she gets everything
right, so she rattles off the usual ingredients—
pork, veal, beef, and so on—though when he walks away,
she hamsters back to my table and puts
her mouth to my ear. "Mint," she says. "The secret is mint."

I CAN

Just then a log snaps in the fireplace and we jump: "Meg
and I race upstairs," says our host, "our hearts in our throat."
They're new parents, see, and dying to have an evening

to themselves, but they just got to town and don't know
any young people, and then they hear of a church babysitting
service, so they call up, and a grandmotherly type appears

that very evening, and they go out and see a movie and have
dinner, and when they come home, she's sitting on the couch.
How'd it go? they say. Fine, she says. Such a lovely girl!

Oh! they say. You must not have changed him or you'd know
he's a boy. The sitter is quiet for a moment and then says,
He may have been a boy before, but he's a girl now.

What must it have been like to be in that moment. Or any
moment. Once, when I loved someone I knew I'd never
have, I was sad and happy all the time, as though I was being

lashed till I bled while looking at the most beautiful art
in the world and listening to the most beautiful music.
Your story is all you have: to think your life will be good

because you are good is like thinking the bull won't toss you
on his horns because you don't eat meat. In the worst years
of Stalin's terror, someone sees the poet Akhmatova

outside the Leningrad prison and says, "Can you describe this?"
and the poet says, "I can." They race upstairs, the new parents,
but the baby is fine, so they come back down, and the sitter

is gone. Come to find out she'd been put away before
for threatening children with scissors and that the kindhearted
church folk knew this, but she'd been through counseling,

so they figured, oh, well, everybody deserves a second chance.
How many times has this man told this story,
how many times has he felt that much pain, felt that alive.

IV

MARY WEISS OF THE SHANGRI-LAS EXPLAINS IT ALL TO YOU

DEAR CHESTNUTS, FRENCH BABIES, STATUES, AND BEES

Luxembourg Gardens, Paris

Ow! You hurt when you hit me: it's the spikes, sure, but also
the height you fall from. Yet I love the way you always split
into the same four pieces, the hull in thirds and then the nut.

What's with the spikes, though? I know: so a dog won't eat you
and take you home in his belly or a baby pick you up and throw
you at another baby and miss so that you land in the street

and are crushed by a passing car. Most French babies
are lazy, though some are not: you hard workers get behind
your own strollers and push them, head down, one leg

stretched out behind you, elbows locked as you strain like Sisyphus;
over the years, your destiny will take on muscle and sinew,
and even now it readies itself to roll backwards, flattening

you into a longer, thinner version of your baby self looking down
at your own baby, but, hey, at least you're trying! Whereas
these statues are shiftless or maybe just smart—stay up on

those pedestals, boys! It's not always so great down here.
As many of you are women as men, though: Margaret of Anjou,
Louise of Savoy, Anne Marie Louise of Orléans. Whoever

thought Louise would be such a popular name for queens?
Louise is a name for the lunchroom lady or your mom,
as is Blanche of Castile. It's a good thing you were born

queens, because you wouldn't have been able to vote
for yourselves till 1945. The babies I like most look like
cookies; you're the ones with round heads and pug

noses, as though a baker stamped you out of cookie dough
and put you in an oven and pulled you out with a wooden
paddle when you were done. You're all drunk: you lurch

from side to side with your mouths open, and you cry when you
don't get your way. Some of you will be drunks when you
grow up, and sooner or later, you'll all scream. Scream,

you screamers—let's hear it! You'll really scream if a bee
stings your little asses: here in the southeast corner
of the garden is the bee city, and look, here's the shop

where I can buy honey from the bees, or rather from the people
who handle you bees' money for you—imagine knowing
the tree that became this piece of paper or the dinosaur

that was the oil that lit Paris last night! Most of you live
in one of eighteen houses with hexagonal roofs and metal balls
on top, and there's a fountain in the middle for water

and bee chat. For the rest of you, there are plain wooden
boxes. You must be the bad bees. What did you do,
sting somebody? Maybe you stole from the other bees.

If so, shame on you! Quit acting like wasps. Though if you
sting a baby, that's just your job. When you babies are older,
you'll have more to scream about, but you'll be too

embarrassed to scream then, so you might as well do it now.
Some of you statues are imaginary, like Manon Lescaut,
lifesize before a column on which Massenet appears

only in relief—whew! Some are animals: stags, does, lions.
Some, like José María de Heredia, don't have French names
but are French. Some of you are unknown: the rain has washed

away your names. You remind me of myself, not that I don't
know who I am, but nobody else does. Hawthorne didn't
like you, any of you. He said you statues don't move,

which means he must not have seen you by moonlight,
but who has? The garden closes every day at sunset.
On her way out, a happy baby lifts her hand to wave

at the wheelchair people who wave back or try to.
A happy baby is a public service and gets an ice cream.
Ow! Soon men will be selling chestnuts on street corners.

Christmas wouldn't be the same without you chestnuts,
even though you smell better than you taste.
I know, I'll buy a bag of you and throw you away.

IF YOU WERE JOHN RILEY

This didn't happen to you, but it would have if your name
were John Riley and you had joined the army in 1845
with thousands of other Irishmen who couldn't land
any other job but then found yourself fighting your co-religionists
in Mexico even as you were being starved and beaten

by Protestant officers who called you "hairy ape," "Papist,"
"Paddy." So off you go with several hundred equally
disillusioned sons of the Green Isle to form the Batallón
de San Patricio and fight on the Mexican side. And since
you've come this far with me, reader, let me ask you

two questions: (1) Is that a good story or what, which isn't
really a question, and (2) Is truth stranger than fiction?
Answer: It depends on the fiction. Balzac, Flaubert?
Not so strange; pretty workaday, pretty routine.
But Dumas and Dickens? Those are the fellows to go

to for your big bow-wow moments, your sudden intakes
of breath, your hey-wait-a-minutes, not to mention
your there-but-for-the-grace-of-Gods. Or take *Pygmalion*,
where Professor Higgins, who is going to India to meet
Colonel Pickering, runs into Pickering in Covent Garden,

the colonel having come to London to meet him.
Or Jean Anouilh's *Eurydice*, in which the lovers see each
other for the first time in a train station; had a child cried
or a bird flown overhead, one or both might have
glanced away, and there'd be no story. Fair enough,

but isn't the real-life encounter between Mick Jagger
and Keith Richards more delicious than anything
a pair of playwrights might have dreamed up? It's 1960,
and the two teenagers meet at Dartford Station,
and Mick is carrying albums by Chuck Berry and Muddy

Waters, and Keith says, Oh, you dig those cats, too,
huh? and they board the same train to London,
the Rolling Stones are born, and music is changed
forever. Years later, another band, Dire Straits, would
sing, "Everybody's looking for / Somebody's arms

to fall into." Ha, ha! They didn't mean Mick and Keith,
but they might as well have, since those two cuddled
like kittens when the going was good and fell to
clawing and spitting at each other when the going
got even better and are still together after fifty years,

like many another grumpy old married couple.
In 1847, the St. Patrick's Brigade was defeated
by their former comrades in arms, and John Riley,
along with six others, was stripped to the waist
and given fifty blows with a rawhide lash—fifty-nine

for Riley when the officer in charge lost count.
Then each was branded on the cheek with a "D"
for "deserter," though Riley's D was upside down,
so they branded him the right way on the other cheek.
After the war, he returns to the Mexican army

as a colonel and then begins to slowly disappear
from history, though an American dragoon claims later
that Riley married a rich and beautiful Mexican woman
and raised a loving family. Is that possible? I know
you believe it, reader, whether it's true or not.

This poem's almost over, and you've come this far,
so you've already bought in the way people do when
they start reading something and follow it all the way
through to its conclusion, and while most of us postmodern
folk are more than a little leery of the happy-ever-after

ending, you wouldn't want me to leave you with a raw
back and two branded cheeks, would you, so let's just
say you're moseying through a plaza in Hermosillo
or Nogales when suddenly you look up to see a woman
looking out over her balcony, and she sees you

and smiles, and here the poem's going to have to refer
to yet another fictional work because, if a writer
has already made your point better than you ever could,
then why not let him or her do the talking, and here
I'm thinking of, not Shaw or Anouilh or any of your other

top-shelf authors mentioned earlier, but the J. D. Salinger
whose story "A Girl I Knew" has a narrator who says
of the girl in the title, "she wasn't doing a thing
that I could see except standing there, leaning
on the balcony railing, holding the universe together."

ALL ART IS THE BLUES

Everything makes my students sad. Songs, movies,
boyfriends, girlfriends: me, too, probably, with my downer diet of quality
literature, almost all of which ends with maiming,
death, abandonment, failed love, sexual betrayal, someone throwing
herself off a parapet, someone else walking into one
body of water or another and never walking out. So whose fault is it,

mine or someone else's? One girl came crying to me after
reading *Revolutionary Road* and said, does everyone have affairs?
Only in books and movies, I replied. You don't
have to have affairs in real life; a lot of people don't. Besides, there are
worse things in life than affairs, like death. Also, who
wants to see a movie about a woman making school lunches and going

to yoga class or a man who puts on a clean shirt every
morning and takes the bus to town and whose most questionable act
is to sip a third glass of Scotch as he sorts nails in
the garage instead of stopping at two? Look, I say: you know what
the blues are? No, the blues is *not* a bunch of old
toothless guys singing about hard work, low pay, the evils of drink,

and that little old gal's treachery. All art is the blues.
Or at least the best art is. Art showcases pain, perfidy, the breakdown
of the body: art does all that for you so you don't
have to do it yourself. Take a Puccini opera. You don't have to die
spitting blood into a handkerchief—let Mimi
cough her lungs up instead! Or a country song. You don't have

to go to jail. Johnny Cash went to jail for you,
for us all. Dante went to hell for us, and if that doesn't make you
feel better, I don't know what will. Dante was

almost killed at the Battle of Campaldino, but when he wasn't,
        he said, "I had great fear, and at last great joy."
That's the difference between the beautiful and the sublime,

        says top English philosopher Edmund Burke:
the beautiful is small, smooth, delicate, whereas the sublime is vast,
        rugged, massive. It's beautiful to paddle your
canoe in the river, sublime to go over a waterfall. If someone
        said, "There's a kitty in the other room,"
you'd say, "Aw! A kitty!" whereas if they said, "There's a tiger,"

        you'd say, "Oh, help, a tiger! Run, everybody—
don't let it get the baby!" Or maybe "don't let it get my baby!"
        or "don't let it get me!" Why do we call the people
we love "baby"? I don't mean "babe," as in "she's a total babe,"
        but "baby," as in helpless newborn?
I know, it's because when we call somebody baby, we're saying

        they're innocent, that they've never known
anyone before us. And they haven't! Our love washes them clean.
        You promise someone you'll walk with them
always, that should a hand slip free, you'll wait, and if you are
        the one who falls behind, then the other will wait
for you. What do you mean, you have to say goodbye—didn't we

        just set out? It's as though the earth itself were
breathing, and the spray rolls up like smoke from a burning city.
        Where are you? I love you to death, also
to pieces. You can't leave me! Think about how much we love
        each other. And remember, Puccini loves
you, too, and so does Johnny Cash. Why else would they write

those masterpieces? Those masterpieces
didn't write themselves, you know. And Arthur Conan Doyle
and the Brontë sisters and Keats and Jane
Austen: they'll be with you always. Marcel Proust. Allen Ginsberg!
Langston Hughes, Virginia Woolf. Come on in,
everybody. Look, the whole world is shaking with love. It won't stop.

SPACE DOGS

And now for this week's question: what do Henry James,
Malcolm X, Sigmund Freud, Charlie Chaplin, Helen Keller,
Orson Welles, and Mark Twain have in common?
That's right: none of them think Shakespeare wrote his plays.

I'm ashamed of you, Mark Twain! The others were snobs,
but you should have known better. You didn't have any more
university training than he did, nor did Whitman, Keats,
and Dickens, for that matter. Look at me: I have a PhD,

and I bet people won't be watching my plays four hundred
years from now, especially since I've never written any.
When the Russians chose dogs for their space program,
do you think they picked thoroughbreds? Hell, no!

They got their dogs off city streets, figuring a pooch
hardened by cold and hunger would be a lot more likely
to survive a trip to outer space. The first one, Laika,
had a white streak in her hair, and for a while there was

a Laika haircut. Can you imagine? Here are all these
beautiful Svetlanas and Irinas, who have worked all
their adult lives to not look like dogs, now having their
hair styled so as to resemble Laika. Then there were

Belka and Strelka, also mixed breeds, like Laika,
and as tough as she was, too. Street dogs were also
cheaper: "Comrade Lab Technician, go to Gorky Park
and grab me a mutt! Two, maybe, depending on how

big they are." I wonder how many great writers you could
stuff into a Soviet space capsule. You could wedge
a couple of Keatses in there, since he was a little fellow,
but only one Whitman, since he was a big guy,

or at least he said he was. Wouldn't it be wonderful
to have all these great poets whirling around overhead,
shooting off sparks and smoke like Fourth of July
fireworks, like the Crackling Palm, the Silver Willow,

Dancing Butterfly, Round Red Dahlia? Pow! There goes
William Blake. Bam—hey, that's Emily Dickinson
up there! And there goes Elizabeth Bishop in an elegant,
silvery arc. Let's make sure we follow directions:

place on a flat surface. Have water handy. Alcohol
and fireworks do not mix. Oh, the hell with all that—
fire it up! Zoom, there she goes, or he, tomorrow's
great poet today, and you were there when it happened.

WHAT TO CALL IT

The two most prestigious journals about nature
and science are called *Nature* and *Science*, so why isn't
there a magazine called *Poetry*? Oh, that's right, there is.
Not that it's the best poetry magazine, although everybody
wants to be in it, probably because it's called *Poetry*

but mainly because everybody wants to be in it.
Thing about poetry is that it's good anyway or maybe
I should say good anywhere, whether it appears
in the magazine named after itself or not. Even bad
poetry is good, if you know what I mean. To say

a poem is bad is like saying a person is ugly,
not that there aren't plenty of ugly people out there.
Maybe we should say so-and-so is not beautiful yet,
just as we say, "You should work on your poem more"
and "What a promising beginning! Now you might

want to take out these four stanzas and fix the end,
and I think it needs a better title, don't you?" just
the way you might say to an ugly person, "Look
how fat I got over the holidays! I think I'm gonna
start walking in the morning—wanna come?"

or "My brother-in-law had the same problem till
he saw a plastic surgeon, and now the women
can't keep their hands off him." Are you looking
at yourself in the mirror now, reader, and thinking,
"I hope he's not talking about me." Well,

of course not, just as I hope you wouldn't
be so judgmental toward the undersigned! As for
that last poem of yours, I think it's quite fine, really,
the sort of thing you might want to bundle with
three or four others and send to *Poetry*. After all,

your poem is rather like this one: not perfect, perhaps,
but many of the world's great artists let a certain
roughness define their work. Why, Buddy Holly
hiccups all the way through his songs, and Jack White
of the White Stripes didn't want drummer Meg White

to practice because he thought the music sounded
better the more primitive it was. As it says in
Proverbs 14:4: "Where no oxen are, the crib
is clean, but much increase is by the strength
of the ox." Here's another example: the Winged

Victory of Samothrace was positioned so viewers saw
only its left side, the drapery of which was depicted
with great care, while on the statue's right side,
which you wouldn't see unless you walked around
back, the folds are fewer and roughly hewn.

That's what we poets do, isn't it—go around
behind the poem and look for the rough parts
and smooth some of them out, sure, just as we
leave others in. I'll do the same: I'll pick four
poems that are alike enough so as to appear

that they emerged from a single mind, that is,
mine, yet sufficiently different that there's some
variety there, some hint that the single mind
which produced these poems doesn't just run
in one direction but has little side tracks, trunk lines

that flow to the east and west yet eventually
return to the main road, thereby suggesting that
the whole is a rich and storied enterprise, a land
with its own people—peoples, really, of different
tribes and tongues—as well as farms, factories,

schools, businesses, governmental buildings,
animals both domestic and wild. Think of it:
all that in just four poems! Why, I'll send them
off this afternoon. Not this one, though.
I want to work on it a little more.

MY LOUSY SAINT

Try not to be dissatisfied with organized religion, reader.
It works for the people who believe in it, and it offers
many satisfactions to those who don't. Take me:
at the little church on the top of the hill in Fiesole,
a brother of the Franciscan order is just coming off his shift
at a perpetual prayer vigil and pauses when he sees me

and smiles, so I ask him why he and the others pray all night.
That's when the devil's out, he says. Good answer, yes?
How I loved the Church as a boy: the Latin mass, the incense,
the guilt, the certainty that my enemies would roast in hell,
the statuary and stained-glass windows. You can imagine
how excited I was when I came across a calendar of saints,

one for each day, though the saint for my birthday
was not Michael or George or Gabriel with a sword and shield
or at least a trumpet but Saturninus, whose unpronounceable
name just looked dumb to a 12-year-old eager for hunky male
role models who stopped wild animals in their tracks,
parted seas, brought the dead back to life. All Saturninus

did was piss off a bunch of pagan priests in Toulouse
because they stopped receiving messages from their gods
whenever he was in the neighborhood, so they subjected
him to "a great variety of indignities," according to the old
chronicles, and had him dragged by a wild bull until dead.
The chronicles also say he went by the name of Cernín,

Sadurní, Sadurninho, Sarnin, Satordi, Saturdi, Saturnin,
Saturnino, Serenín, Sernin, and Zernin, as though the old
chroniclers themselves didn't know how to pronounce

a word that sounds more like an adenoid condition
than a name. You say Saturninus, I say gesundheit.
But I wasn't mad at you, Saint Saturninus; it's just that

I wanted a marquee-name saint: John the Baptist, say,
or Thomas Becket, or at least one with a cool name,
like Leo the Great. Then there's Joseph Moscati,
Alphonsus Maria de Liguori, Bernardo Scammacca . . .
why do so many saints sound like mafiosi? A really
cool saint would be Saint Margaret of Cortona, patron

of homeless people, midwives, single women, people
who are tempted sexually and who are mentally ill
(not the same group, but think about it), people ridiculed
for their piety, and tertiaries. What are tertiaries? A tertiary
is composed of lay members of a religious order,
that is, men and women who do not live in a monastery

or convent but who wear the habit and participate
in the practices of that order. Everybody wants to belong
to a club, to the Catholic Church, say, or the mafia.
I belong to the biggest club ever, ex-Catholics.
Most of us are good people, I bet, or at least interesting ones.
We should get together and find out. The young Franciscan

who tells me they pray at night because that's when the devil's
out also says the rates are cheaper then, and when I ask what
he means by that, he says it's like long-distance calling:
everybody prays during the day, so at night, there's less traffic.
During the day, he says, students pray for good grades,
women pray for grandchildren. . . . At night, it's just us.

THE CHRONICLE OF HIGHER EDUCATION

As I am waiting to go on stage at commencement,
I shake hands with a gentleman I don't know
and tell him my name, and when he tells me his,
and I ask him what his role is at the university,
he pauses, and his eyes widen in disbelief and he says,
"I'm the athletic director," and then of course I want
to mess with him, so I point down and say, "Here?"
The athletic director is certainly an imposing presence,
unlike, say, German philosopher Martin Heidegger,
who was shy and tiny and had a little pinched mouth
as well as a lifelong aversion to meeting people's eyes,
yet he turned the world on its ear with his innovative
thinking about such matters as being and time.
Even as a child, Heidegger "was the smallest, he was
the weakest, he was the most unruly, he was the most
useless," recalls a friend, "but he was in command
of us all." At my university, the athletic director
is in command of us all, even the president. All
the president does is raise money, all I do is write
poems, and as to the philosophers, who knows
what they are up to these days. Which is the most
important? In a hundred years, it could be me,
if the poems are good enough, though there are no
famous poems about athletic directors. Then again,
the greatest poems are about the littlest things: a bird
for Keats, a flea for John Donne. Walter Whitman,
the failed poet who couldn't hold down a job,
wrote about Walt Whitman, the healthy comrade
and invincible optimist. Did you know that Whitman
wrote a 47,000-word fitness guide under the name
"Mose Velsor"? A graduate student at another university

discovered that on a microfilm that hadn't been
digitized yet. Whitman suggests that we eat meat,
mainly, and wear comfortable shoes, and he warns
against inactivity: "To you, clerk, literary man, sedentary
person, man of fortune, idler, the same advice,"
he declared. "Up!" I wish more poets were as clever
as the professors in the psychology department who
were studying gratitude, so they had young men
and women exchange gift certificates, though
they switched the certificates unbeknownst
to the participants, thus leading a young fellow
to think he's giving a young lady a certificate from
a bookstore, but really it's for acne cream. Ha, ha!
T. S. Eliot said there is good poetry, bad poetry,
and chaos, but there would be less chaos if more poets
followed the advice of Herr Heidegger, who told
Hannah Arendt that he wrote with "the calm rhythm
of a man chopping wood in a forest." Making
your own wood fires is not only exercise of the sort
that Whitman would approve of but also good
domestic economy, since it is an activity that warms you
you twice, once when you chop the wood and once
again when you burn it. Same with poetry. Same
with football! You do it, it's over, you do it again.

ODE TO IGNORANCE

The museum guide says, "This statue is from Delphi,"
and a woman in our group says, "Yes, where they make
the china," and the guide says, "Actually, you're thinking
of Delft, not Delphi, which is somewhat to the north—
in the Netherlands, actually, and not in Greece at all,"
and I think, Ignorance, my old friend, how dare you
work for others! Why do you waste your gifts

on those who don't recognize their value? I ran into
Salman Rushdie once and said, "Mr. Rushdie, did you
know that Tallahassee is the only city in the world
that contains the name of Allah?" and he said, "Well,
there are many cities in the world and many languages,
so perhaps that is not the case." True, but from there
we went on to speak of many a subject and fleet the time

carelessly, and how would we have done that were
it not for my blunder, unless, of course, I'm right?
Speaking of literary figures, who would have guessed
that Gregory Corso is not only buried in the Protestant
Cemetery in Rome but is also just one grave away
from Shelley? Had I known that beforehand, I would
never have gone to that august burial ground, but now

I think of the two of them lying near each other every day,
the great Beat poet and the doomed Romantic who would
have loathed or perhaps adored each other in real life—
we'll never know, will we? Once I saw a card in a gift shop
that said, "Your work is to discover your world and then
with all your heart give yourself to it," which admirable
sentiment was attributed to the Buddha, though it doesn't

sound like the Buddha I know. The Buddha I know is a lot
grumpier than that; he believes that ours is a world
of suffering and that our task is to reduce that suffering
as much as possible through prayer and meditation,
not erase it entirely and sit around eating popsicles
and thinking how groovy we are, so I look up the saying
on line, and sure enough, there's a site called Fake Buddha

Quotes, of which this is one. Why the Buddha, though?
I know, because he deals in paradox, so almost anything
you attribute to him will make sense or seem to. Simone
de Beauvoir herself liked to conclude her debates with Sartre
by saying, "I'm no longer sure *what* I think, nor whether
I can be said to think at all," and she was Simone de Beauvoir,
though I think that, like me, she knew that she would get

farther in this world by laying claim to how little she knew
rather than how much, also that, again like me, she was
proud of her knowledge, such as it was, but also of the casks,
barrels, buckets, tubs, butter churns, hogsheads, firkins,
rundlets, butts, pipes, tuns, and puncheons of half-knowledge,
bewilderment, mental incapacity, obtuseness, benightedness,
and fog that she possessed as well and that stood her

in excellent stead during her colloquies with Monsieur Sartre,
than whom she was a much better writer. Ignorance,
not everyone is smart enough to learn from you.
Not everyone is patient enough to climb the slope
of your great mountain, bathe in your spring, drink
from your holy river, hover over your abyss,
breathe your vapors, hear what you're really saying.

MARY WEISS OF THE SHANGRI-LAS EXPLAINS IT ALL TO YOU

A student I haven't seen for months stops by to say hello,
        and she's wearing a sundress, and when she gets up to leave,
I see she has a tattoo on her shoulder, so I say, "Hold on
        a sec, let me take a look," and when I see
it says, "Poetry is not reflection; it is refraction," I say, "I like that,"

and she says, "You should. You said that in the first class
        I took from you." It's times like this that I impress myself.
Not for long, though: the more interesting thing to think
        about is not my excellence but the process whereby
we turn our experiences into art that moves others, to do, for example,

what Mary Weiss of the Shangri-Las did when she sang "Leader
        of the Pack," recalling "I had enough pain in me, at the time,
to pull off anything. And to get into it, and sound—believable."
        We believe you, Mary. Mainly because you're so
restrained when you sing that song, as though you're not really bothered

by the fact that the love of your life has just roared away
        on his motorcycle only to be turned into a pile of hamburger
somewhere out on Highway 30. Restraint: that's the thing,
        isn't it? Discipline. Self-command. The more
he wrote songs, the more Burt Bacharach's music took odd turns,

became clipped and staccato, offbeat. "One-level records
        always made me a little bit uncomfortable after a while,"
he says. "They stayed at one intensity. It kind of beats you up,
        you know? It's like a smile. If you have a great
smile, you use it quick, not all the time." Burt Bacharach sounds

like a smart guy. You have to trust the listener to pick up
on the little thing, to change and color it
until it's the biggest part of the song, even though it's the smallest.
And the least true, maybe, in the factual sense.
I don't remember telling my class about reflection and refraction,

but if I did, I was freeing the students from the absolute need
to reflect their world and telling them that
what they refracted was theirs to make, that you can disconnect
your image from reality. Mary Weiss says,
"The recording studio was the place where you could really release

what you're feeling without everybody looking at you." And the poem
is the place where we poets do the same. Everybody
listened to Mary Weiss—that song was number one
on the pop charts in 1964—and we poets, too, want
to lose ourselves in our early poem drafts so we can write and rewrite

and revise until the poem is so good that everybody loves it,
whether or not they actually end up doing so. When I ask
my former student what other tattoos she has, she says
that's the only one, and when I say, "Wow,
it means that much to you, huh?" she says no, it really hurt.

MORE THAN THIS

When you tell me that a woman is visiting the grave
of her college friend and she's trying not to get irritated
at the man in the red truck who keeps walking back and forth
and dropping tools as he listens to a pro football
game on the truck radio, which is much too loud, I start
to feel as though I know where this story is going,
so I say *Stop, you're going to make me cry.*
How sad the world is. When young men died in the mud
of Flanders, the headmaster called their brothers out
of the classroom one by one, but when the older brothers
began to die by the hundreds every day, they simply handed
the child a note as he did his lessons, and of course the boy
wouldn't cry in front of the others, though at night
the halls were filled with the sound of schoolboys sobbing
for the dead, young men only slightly older than themselves.
Yet the world's beauty breaks our hearts as well:
the old cowboy is riding along and looks down
at his dog and realizes she died a long time ago
and that his horse did as well, and this makes him
wonder if he is dead, too, and as he's thinking this,
he comes to a big shiny gate that opens onto a golden
highway, and there's a man in a robe and white wings,
and when the cowboy asks what this place is, the man tells
him it's heaven and invites him in, though he says animals
aren't allowed, so the cowboy keeps going till he comes
to an old rusty gate with a road full of weeds and potholes
on the other side and a guy on a tractor, and the guy
wipes his brow and says you three must be thirsty,
come in and get a drink, and the cowboy says okay,
but what is this place, and the guy says it's heaven,
and the cowboy says then what's that place down

the road with the shiny gate and the golden highway,
and when the guy says oh, that's hell, the cowboy
says doesn't it make you mad that they're pretending
to be you, and the guy on the tractor says no,
we like it that they screen out the folks who'd desert
their friends. You tell me your friend can't take it
any more, and she turns to confront the man
who's making all the noise, to beg him to leave her alone
with her grief, and that's when she sees that he's been
putting up a Christmas tree on his son's grave
and that he's grieving, too, but in his own way,
one that is not better or worse than the woman's,
just different, the kind of grief that says the world
is so beautiful, that it will give you no peace.

A WORLD IN WHICH THESE THINGS HAPPEN

The Ionian Sea, noon to early evening

Driving onto the ferry at Patra isn't difficult
because there's nowhere to go except onto the ferry,
though once you're on, the trouble starts: the guy
who is guiding you into place not only wants you to back

your car into a space exactly the size of the car itself
but also wants you to watch him, not the cars
on either side, so he stands facing you with his hands
on an invisible steering wheel that he turns all the way

to the right, and you don't know whether that means
you should turn to the right, which is his left, or whether
he wants you to think of him as a mirror
image and turn the wheel to the left, a choice that would be

clear if he were to face away from you, though
then he couldn't see you and the car would never
get parked or at least parked correctly,
which it does eventually, meaning you're free now to go up

on deck and look at all the other ships as you chug out
of the harbor, and as you do, you wonder if these
beat-up freighters have something on
them they shouldn't—a duffel full of heroin, a shipping

container loaded with AKs, a body—but even if they
don't, you're no more the kind of person who wants
to live in a world where such things are
unimaginable than you are the kind who, when the car ferry

reaches Vathi, doesn't do everything he did to get on board
in the first place, only this time in reverse, so that
by now you're more than ready to take a little
something at the port café where the only empty seat is next

to a guy who's maybe eighty and has a houndstooth fedora
and the kind of tinted glasses favored (at least in movies)
by Baltic spies, and after a few minutes,
you're absolutely certain that he is about to say *I understand*

the cheese pies are excellent here in Vathi and you'll
wait a bit and say *Yes but they are even better*
in Frikes and he'll say *The oracle speaks, yet*
the priest cannot shoe his horse and you'll say *My wife's uncle*

is sick because the highway is green and finally he'll say
Just tell us where the stolen art is buried or *When*
does the invasion begin or *Who abducted*
the prime minister, and that's when you realize how little

you understand anything about anything, which
is okay, because if you had to understand everything,
the world wouldn't work at all, though
you're fairly certain that if one part of this endless day

were to change, then the whole day would change
and you as well, that you might even disappear,
that he might say *fruit pies*
instead of *cheese pies* and poof, like that, you're gone.

NOTES

In a 2011 interview in *Time,* Sting says, "I don't think there's such a thing as composition in pop music. I think what we do in pop music is collate. It's like folk music. It makes copyright a bit interesting and difficult. I'm a good collator." I hope the readers will find some original lines in *More Than This,* but Sting is right: every new work of art is a tiny point at the top of a pyramid whose base is immeasurable. In my case, that pyramid is made of these blocks: the literary masters from whom I freely borrow, from Shakespeare and Keats to Whitman and Ginsberg; the Bible; the great songwriters and singers of the last 150 years, from Puccini and Verdi to Little Richard and "girl group" vocalists like Mary Weiss of the Shangri-Las; the symphonic masters who gave me the idea for this book's four-part structure; my students, who teach me without meaning to; and the thousands of unnamed strangers I've bumped into in bars and barbershops in towns and cities from Attapulgus and Sopchoppy to Paris and Rome, honest ordinary people who are, like all of us, extraordinary (and not always honest).

None of what I have done would be possible without Florida State University, my sole employer for my entire adult life and the provider of a biweekly paycheck as well as the numerous attaboys that are just as essential.

Then there's Barbara Hamby. Asking Barbara out was the smartest thing I've ever done. The author of award-winning poetry and prose, Barbara is so accomplished that I wasn't surprised when a publicist who was writing a story about her asked me if I was drawn to Barbara because of her brains and ability, but the truth is that I couldn't keep my hands off her. Barbara has also read every word I have written and helped me to realize which ones work and which don't. What George Martin was to the Beatles, Barbara is to me. In medicine, a second opinion is a good idea. In art, it's essential.

* * *

The following poems in *More Than This* have back stories that deserve airing.

"Big Meal with Gioachino Rossini"

The James Bond movie referred to is *The Man with the Golden Gun,* though I took the funhouse mirror reference from Garth Stein's novel *The Art of Racing in the Rain.* The briar patch image which presents a contrasting view of the nature of truth is from Pete Seeger, who says it's a simile his father was fond of.

"Tony Bennett sings 'Smile' for You"

Francine Christophe tells her own story in a number of widely distributed videos, any of which can be found by entering her name into the YouTube search engine.

"Always Something There to Remind Me"

The young woman in this poem is Nidžara Ahmetăsević, who survived her wartime experiences and became a journalist. Her story is told in Sebastian Junger's *Tribe: On Homecoming and Belonging.*

"You Found That Thing You Lost"

This is the poem that is closest to a pure collation of the type Sting mentions. I asked on Facebook what items people would squirrel away for doomsday, and every item listed here is one suggested by Facebook friends, the majority of whom I don't really know. The voices that decry social media are legion; mine is not one of them.

"We Three Kings"

The source for the Henry Tandey story is an August 4, 2014, article on www.bbc.com. In the course of a 1938 visit to Hitler's Bavarian retreat the Berghof, British Prime Minister Neville Chamberlain noticed a painting depicting a scene from a World War I battle in 1914. The soldier who is depicted carrying a comrade to safety in the painting's foreground was said to be Private Tandey. Hitler told Chamberlain the soldier had pointed a gun at him but decided to spare him.

Ample doubt is cast on this story in the article. Private Tandey acknowledged having spared German soldiers at that particular battle but always made a point of saying he needed more information before he could confirm that one of those soldiers was Hitler. Whether or not it was Tandey who lowered his weapon, Hitler himself believed he was spared by a British soldier who had become sick of killing.

"More Than This"

This poem appeared originally in both the print and online issues of *Rattle* in 2016. Later I learned that it was that journal's most popular post of the year, having been read by some 50,000 viewers. It also appeared in the 2016 Pushcart Prize anthology, which is when I began to think that the title of my next book was being handed to me.

The note accompanying "More Than This" in *Rattle* reads: "A lot of my poems are braids I make of found materials; my contribution is to figure out what the different parts have in common and then unite them tonally. In this case, there are three threads. My barber told me the cowboy story. The one about the English schoolboys was told in class by a student who'd read it somewhere. But I no longer remember where I encountered the story set in the cemetery, the one that begins and ends the poem. Oh, and this braid is drenched in the bittersweet hues of the great Jack Gilbert; I fell hard for him just before I began writing this."

Since then I've learned that the source of the cemetery story is Jessica Strawser's "An Extra Angel on Top of the Tree," which appeared in the *New York Times* on December 11, 2014. When I realized this, I wrote Ms. Strawser. We're friends now, and her novel *Almost Missed You* was published recently; you should read it. And I should mention two other influences, both musical. The first is, of course, "More Than This," the lush Roxy Music song about love and uncertainty. And then taken as a whole, Leonard Cohen's songs say again and again that when love is broken, that's not entirely a bad thing, because its pieces fly everywhere.